The *NEW* LAWN EXPERT

Dr. D.G.Hessayon

Enlarged edition: 150,000 copies

Published 1997
by Expert Books
a division of Transworld Publishers Ltd

All Editions & Reprints: 3,312,000 copies

TRANSWORLD PUBLISHERS LTD
61–63 Uxbridge Road, London W5 5SA

Distributed in the United States
by Sterling Publishing Co. Inc.,
387 Park Avenue South,
New York, NY 10016–8810

Distributed in Canada by
Cavendish Books Inc.,
Unit 5, 801 West 1st Street,
North Vancouver, B.C. V7P 1A4

EXPERT BOOKS

Contents

Reproduction by Spot On Repro Ltd, Perivale, Middlesex
Printed and bound in Great Britain by Jarrold & Sons Ltd, Norwich

ISBN 0 903505 48 7

CHAPTER 1

INTRODUCTION

We are told that the size of the average garden is about 2000 sq. ft, but the difference between one garden and another may be enormous. Tiny courtyard gardens abound in the cities and there are vast estates scattered in rural areas, but they all rather surprisingly have one feature in common. The owner almost always considers it either impractical, unappealing or impossible to cover the whole area with a mixture of flowers, trees, shrubs and/or vegetables with exposed earth between the plants.

This means that there is a universal need for some permanent form of ground cover in which beds, borders, rockery, greenhouse, pond etc. can be set. Generally more than one type of ground cover is used, but in most gardens the main type is the grass lawn.

As defined later the grass lawn is an area covered with closely-knit turf grasses — this grassy surface is regularly mown to keep it smooth and it is capable of standing up to a reasonable amount of foot traffic. Some types of lawn can tolerate the heavy wear of regular treading and children's games but others cannot — some look like green velvet whereas others are coarse, uneven and spotted with weeds and moss, but they are all grass lawns.

For most of us a garden is just not a garden without a lawn and on the large areas surrounding grand country houses nearly all of the land may be down to grass lawns, but the position is rather different in the average garden. Here we want to see flowers and shrubs from the windows and we may also want a place for the greenhouse and vegetables, so it is not surprising that only half of the average plot is down to mown grass. There is another reason for limiting the amount of turf in the garden —

grass is not an all-purpose ground cover. For paths, drives and other areas subject to very heavy foot or vehicle traffic we must use hard landscaping rather than turf — this calls for non-living material such as stone slabs, bricks, gravel, concrete etc. For covering the bare spaces between shrubs and trees we obviously cannot use grass, and in this situation ground-covering plants are used.

To summarise, there are three ground-covering materials which are commonly used in the average garden — lawn grasses, hard landscaping such as paving or gravel, and ground-covering plants. The relative amounts used of these three types of ground cover may vary widely from one garden to another. In a tiny garden there may be more hard landscaping than grass lawn, and in the labour-saving garden there will be a large amount of ground-covering planting so as to keep down the weeds between the woody plants and reduce the need for watering in dry weather.

Apart from these three basic ground-cover types there are four others which have a part to play in certain situations. The most important of these alternative ground covers is the meadow — an area of grassland which is cut only occasionally. This is a feature of the large garden where it would not be practical nor even desirable to have all the grass closely shorn. As described in Chapter 9 the meadow can also have a role in the smaller garden and so can its more sophisticated relative which is arousing much interest these days — the wildflower meadow in which wildflower seeds are sown. The remaining two types of ground cover are the synthetic lawn composed of plastic carpeting and the non-grass lawn composed of chamomile, thyme or other creeping plant. Neither of these types is really practical, so this brief introduction to ground-covering materials has ranged from the hardly ever absent to the hardly ever seen.

7 WAYS TO COVER THE GROUND

GRASS LAWN — pages 5–100

SYNTHETIC LAWN — page 115

MEADOW — pages 106–108

WILDFLOWER MEADOW — pages 109–114

HARD LANDSCAPING — pages 118–120

GROUND COVER PLANTS — pages 121–125

NON-GRASS LAWN — pages 116–117

CHAPTER 2

THE GRASS LAWN

Nobody loves a lawn book. For many garden owners it is a great delight to browse through books on flowers, flowering shrubs and roses. Their pages are filled with glossy pictures of beautiful blooms, but the pages of a lawn guide are filled with practical instructions and pictures of weeds, equipment and brown patches.

So nobody loves a lawn book, but everyone loves a lawn. The expanse of green turf around the house sets the scene for the whole garden. In summer the lawn unites the bright and varied bits of scenery such as the flower beds, shrub border and rockery. In winter its role is reversed — it brings greenness and life to an empty stage. Home owners realise this and want a first rate lawn, a lawn that looks like a bowling green. This brings us to the first basic lesson concerning lawns. There are two types of first rate lawn, not one. The bowling green type is the luxury grade, but this green velvet is not a good choice for the average garden. It needs a regular routine of feeding, weeding, aerating and top dressing as well as cutting every few days in summer if it is to remain in good condition. If your turf will have to cope with children's feet, washing lines and occasional neglect then the hard-wearing utility grade is a much better choice.

The difference between these two grades of lawn is due to the nature of the grasses, so it is necessary to pick the right grade when buying seed or turf for a new lawn. This book will tell you what to look for, and how to improve a poor quality luxury-grade lawn by dressing it with the right type of seed.

This book will also show you how to follow the second basic rule — always plan carefully when designing a new lawn or changing the one you have. Your lawn should never be an obstacle course for the mower. An area of grass strewn with isolated trees, island beds, square corners, narrow paths and items of furniture can take twice or three times as long to cut as a well-designed one. If you have time to spare and enjoy the exercise then this may not matter, but remember that you have to cut the lawn for about 30 weeks between spring and autumn, and it's a job not enjoyed by most garden owners.

The third basic rule concerns the mower — the one to buy should be wide enough and powerful enough to tackle your lawn as quickly and easily as possible within your budget, bearing in mind that a mower can be too big for the job in hand as well as too small.

Choosing the right grasses, the right design and the right mower provide the building blocks for a first rate lawn but all will be lost if you don't give it the right care. It is at this stage that a lawn book comes into its own. Here you will find out what to do when something goes wrong. An unsightly problem in the lawn is extremely worrying — everyone can see it and unlike a sickly shrub you can't simply dig it up and replace it. There is no more distressing situation in the whole of gardening than to watch a lawn deteriorate to the point where it is an ugly eyesore, a patchwork quilt of greens and browns. And it is unnecessary as Britain is the home of the Beautiful Lawn. People from overseas often marvel at the quality of our turf, but this is due to our favourable climate for grass and the relative freedom from crippling pests and diseases rather than to any innate native skill. Sadly most lawns are left to fend for themselves apart from a weekly mowing, a splash of chemical if weeds get too bad and a feed if the grass gets too yellow. A lawn needs more — it needs a regular routine of simple tasks and this book will show you what to do.

WHAT THE WORDS MEAN

VERGE
A narrow strip of turf between beds, borders, paths, walls etc.

LAWN
A smooth area of land covered with turf

TURF
A ground cover of grass which is kept mown and which will stand a reasonable amount of traffic

SWARD
Another name for turf

NAP
The description of the lawn surface when all the grass foliage lies in the same direction

WASHBOARDING
A series of corrugations, with the crests about 6–12 in. apart, at right angles to the direction of mowing. For cause and cure, see page 86

BENTS ('SOLDIERS')
Grass stalks which have not been cut by the mower — flowering stems of Perennial Ryegrass are the usual bents seen in a lawn. Remove by cutting off individually with shears. Do not confuse the word with Bent grasses — see page 12

RIBBING
A series of narrow lines of long and short grass, at right angles to the direction of mowing. For cause and cure, see page 86

RAKING

AERATING

SCARIFYING
The vigorous use of a rake or rake-like tool to remove thatch; this job is done in autumn — never in spring. Scarification is also carried out to remove moss after it has been killed by Lawn Sand or a proprietary moss killer

RAKING
The gentle use of a spring-tine rake or similar tool to remove fallen leaves or surface debris and to prevent the build-up of excessive thatch. It is also used to raise the foliage of weeds before mowing

SPIKING
A technique which creates air channels to a depth of at least 3 in. Its purpose is to relieve compaction. In this way drainage is improved and the growth of new roots is stimulated

PRICKING
A technique which creates air channels to a depth of less than 3 in. Its purpose is to break through the surface mat of dead vegetation and help the downward passage of water and fertilizer

THATCH
A layer of fibrous material on top of the soil surface. When it is incorporated with the soil surface, this layer is more properly called a *mat*.
Thatch less than ½ in. thick is useful — it adds springiness and cuts down surface water loss.
Thatch over 1 in. thick is harmful — water penetration is reduced and the likelihood of disease is increased

COMPACTION
Regular mowing and heavy traffic can cause the particles of the soil to squeeze together. This compaction drives out air and root development becomes stifled. The compacted layer seldom exceeds a depth of 3 in. Test for compaction: If you can push a matchstick completely and easily into the soil with the ball of your thumb, the lawn is not compacted

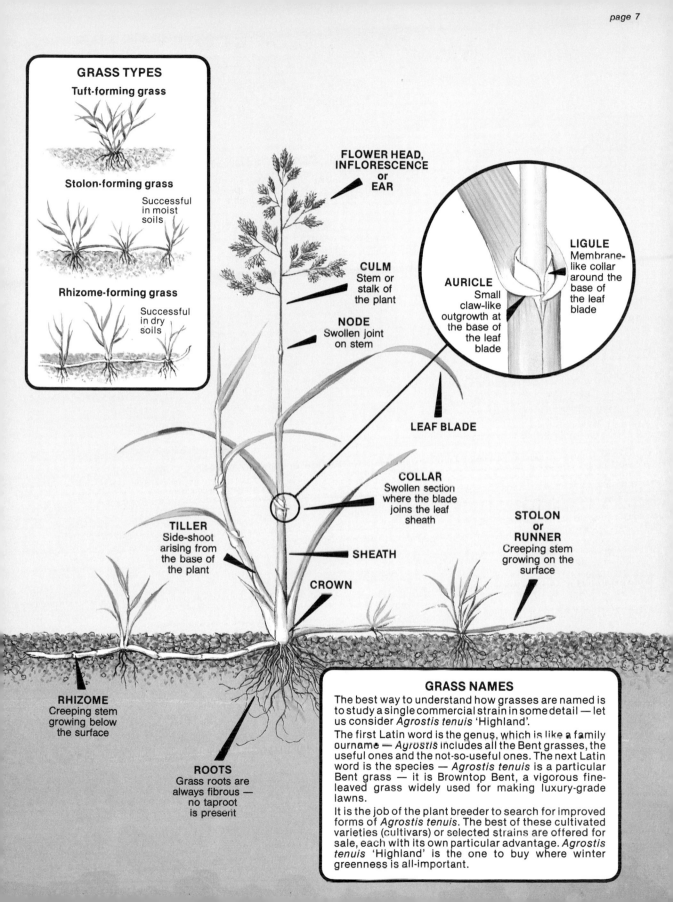

GRASS TYPES

Tuft-forming grass

Stolon-forming grass

Successful in moist soils

Rhizome-forming grass

Successful in dry soils

FLOWER HEAD, INFLORESCENCE or **EAR**

CULM
Stem or stalk of the plant

NODE
Swollen joint on stem

AURICLE
Small claw-like outgrowth at the base of the leaf blade

LIGULE
Membrane-like collar around the base of the leaf blade

LEAF BLADE

COLLAR
Swollen section where the blade joins the leaf sheath

STOLON or **RUNNER**
Creeping stem growing on the surface

TILLER
Side-shoot arising from the base of the plant

SHEATH

CROWN

RHIZOME
Creeping stem growing below the surface

ROOTS
Grass roots are always fibrous — no taproot is present

GRASS NAMES

The best way to understand how grasses are named is to study a single commercial strain in some detail — let us consider *Agrostis tenuis* 'Highland'.

The first Latin word is the genus, which is like a family ourname — *Agrostis* includes all the Bent grasses, the useful ones and the not-so-useful ones. The next Latin word is the species — *Agrostis tenuis* is a particular Bent grass — it is Browntop Bent, a vigorous fine-leaved grass widely used for making luxury-grade lawns.

It is the job of the plant breeder to search for improved forms of *Agrostis tenuis*. The best of these cultivated varieties (cultivars) or selected strains are offered for sale, each with its own particular advantage. *Agrostis tenuis* 'Highland' is the one to buy where winter greenness is all-important.

THE DOS & DON'TS OF LAWN DESIGN

TREES

Maintaining a lawn under a tree which bears a dense canopy of leaves is extremely difficult. Shade, food shortage and water shortage exhaust the grasses and the drip from the edge of the leaf canopy is damaging. The usual result is sparse grass and abundant moss, which may call for re-seeding every year. Tackle the problem by removing the lower branches, watering at the first sign of drought and cutting the grass less frequently than for the rest of the lawn. In autumn spike the turf and re-seed with a proprietary mixture designed for shady sites. If the tree is an oak or beech the best plan may be to give up the struggle. Remove the turf from around the trunk and create a large bed in which bulbs and shade-loving shrubs or perennials can be grown. If you want to plant a tree in or next to the lawn, choose a small-leaved type such as birch or laburnum.

BANKS

Hover and lightweight electric mowers are capable of cutting sloping turf quite easily, so extending the lawn over a bank is practical these days. There are still two rules — the depth of topsoil on the bank must be no less than occurs over the rest of the lawn and the slope must not exceed 30°. If the slope is more than 30°, plant it instead with ground cover plants or transform the bank into a terrace by building a retaining wall.

BULBS

Daffodils heralding in the spring are a welcome sight, but they are a problem in the lawn. The leaves must be left to die down naturally if next year's display is to be satisfactory, but that means leaving the area uncut for several weeks. Obviously bulbs have no place in the first rate lawn as any prolonged period without mowing can lead to turf deterioration. An answer is to plant the daffodils in rough grassland (see page 106), but this is not practical in a small garden. A good alternative is to plant them in the turf under trees — in this situation a delay in mowing will not have a serious effect.

SHAPE & SITE

The shape should be one which appeals to you — do not design a lawn you don't like just because the 'experts' say it is the right thing to do. Good design is a marriage of an attractive shape with an easy-to-care-for shape; an eye-catching lawn which is a nightmare to mow is a bad design. A square or rectangle is the traditional shape, but garden designers feel that a simple irregular outline is more attractive and is easier to mow. Avoid small and fussy curves or awkward corners at all costs. The lawn need not be horizontal — a gentle slope of about 1 in 80 is quite satisfactory. All parts should receive at least some direct sunlight — dense shade is bound to lead to problems. If one corner of the site is very badly drained, use it as a bed for moisture-loving plants rather than as part of the lawn.

POTS & FURNITURE

Heavy seats and large flower pots have no place as permanent features on the lawn. Mowing around them each time you cut the grass is an extra chore, and temporarily moving them while you mow is equally time-consuming. It is much better to site flower tubs and permanent garden furniture elsewhere.

ACCESS

Avoid a restricted access to the lawn as shown in the illustration. Excessive wear and compaction are bound to occur at the entry point and bare patches are inevitable. Screening with walls and fences should be kept to a minimum, but it will be necessary to hide from view unsightly objects such as compost heaps.

PATHS

Paths should not lead directly on to the lawn. The regular traffic on to and off the grass will cause excessive wear and compaction at the point where the turf and path meet. Try to run the path along one side of the lawn, as shown in the illustration. The level of the path should be below the lawn and a grass-free mowing edge should be maintained between them to make mowing and edging easier. There is a wide range of materials available for path-making and the choice is up to you, but do avoid loose chippings. These can easily be kicked on to the lawn and the mower blades may be damaged.

Paths in lawns
Stepping stones set in the lawn will prevent excessive wear along the well-trodden routes. Make sure at all costs that the top of each stone is below the level of the soil surface.

MOWING EDGE

A clear grass-free strip of earth or a mowing strip of slabs or bricks should be maintained all round the lawn — this means that the grass must not extend right up to the base of walls, fences, trees or raised paths. The gap between the lawn and a fence or wall should be wide enough to allow unhindered movement of the mower. Preparing a mowing strip is an extra job to do, but it cuts down or eliminates the need for trimming the edges with shears after mowing. Set the slabs or bricks slightly below the surface of the lawn so that the mower can be taken over the top of the hard surface.

OVERHANGING BRANCHES

In many gardens low-growing branches of trees and shrubs transgress on to the lawn area, and it is no use ignoring the problem by pushing them out of the way each time you mow. You can either trim back the branches or cut back the lawn edge at the base of the tree or shrub.

ISLAND BEDS

The purists feel that flower beds should be kept out of the lawn. It is true that beds in a small lawn will make it look even smaller, and there is no doubt that islands of brightly-coloured flowers breaking up the green surface can look extremely fussy. What the purists forget is that some people *like* their gardens to look fussy and crowded, and so it really is up to you. If, however, you want to follow the rules of good design then keep the following points in mind. Restrict the number of beds to one or two and keep them in proportion to the size of the lawn. Place the bed in a corner rather than in the centre of the lawn and consider planting a stately conifer or other specimen bush or tree rather than a mass of bedding plants. At the time of preparation, seed the whole of the area and cut the beds out after the grass is established.

VERGES

Narrow verges between beds and paths make mowing difficult. They should be at least 3 ft wide.

HOW TO RECOGNISE YOUR LAWN TYPE

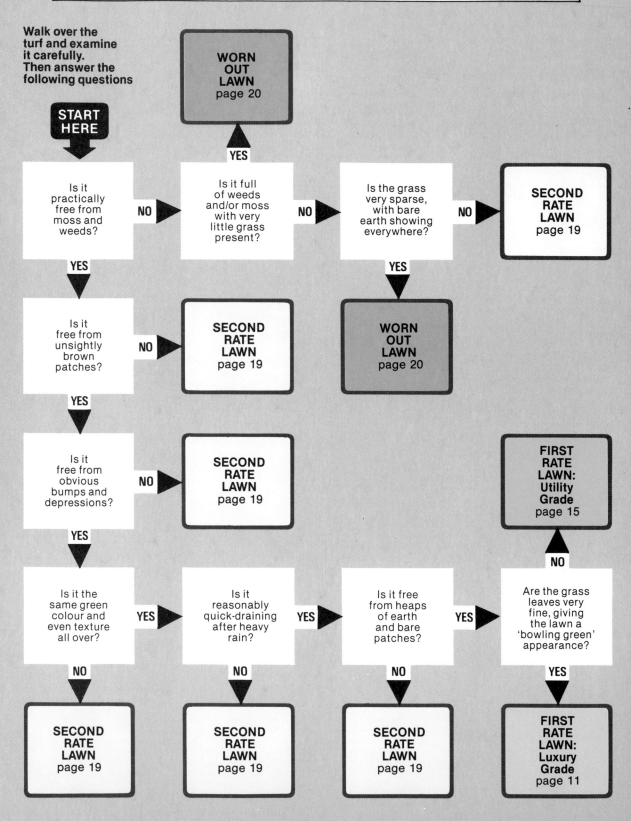

Walk over the turf and examine it carefully. Then answer the following questions

WORN OUT LAWN page 20

START HERE

Is it practically free from moss and weeds? — **NO** → Is it full of weeds and/or moss with very little grass present? — **NO** → Is the grass very sparse, with bare earth showing everywhere? — **NO** → **SECOND RATE LAWN** page 19

YES ↑ (Worn Out Lawn)

YES ↓

Is it free from unsightly brown patches? — **NO** → **SECOND RATE LAWN** page 19

YES ↓ (grass very sparse) → **WORN OUT LAWN** page 20

YES ↓

Is it free from obvious bumps and depressions? — **NO** → **SECOND RATE LAWN** page 19

FIRST RATE LAWN: Utility Grade page 15

YES ↓

Is it the same green colour and even texture all over? — **YES** → Is it reasonably quick-draining after heavy rain? — **YES** → Is it free from heaps of earth and bare patches? — **YES** → Are the grass leaves very fine, giving the lawn a 'bowling green' appearance? — **NO** → **FIRST RATE LAWN: Utility Grade** page 15

NO ↓ → **SECOND RATE LAWN** page 19

NO ↓ → **SECOND RATE LAWN** page 19

NO ↓ → **SECOND RATE LAWN** page 19

YES ↓ → **FIRST RATE LAWN: Luxury Grade** page 11

THE FIRST RATE LAWN: Luxury Grade

There is no mistaking the luxury lawn, with its velvety close pile and 'bowling green' appearance. This velvet look, so beloved by visitors to Britain, is brought about by two factors. Firstly, the turf is composed of fine-leaved compact grasses — the Bents and Fescues; there are no broad-leaved lawn grasses and no Perennial Ryegrass. Secondly, the grass is kept closely and regularly mown at carpet-pile height. In this way the coarser grasses are prevented from taking hold and swamping the fine-leaved varieties.

Here is the classical ornamental lawn, ideal for the area close to the house where it can be seen by all but walked on by very few. If you want your lawn to be a thing of beauty, with its main function to arouse the envy of the neighbours, then this is the turf for you. But be warned — before you rush out with spade and bag of seed to remake your old utility lawn, remember that the luxury lawn has a number of drawbacks and difficulties:

● A luxury lawn will not stand up to very hard wear, such as the feet of children at play or the feet of its owner constantly using it as a pathway to the garage or vegetable plot.

● A luxury lawn will not stand up to neglect in the same way as a tough utility one. You must be prepared for a regular routine of lawn management.

● Seed and turf for a luxury lawn are more expensive than the utility equivalents. The difference between the two grades is greater with turf than with seed.

● Establishment of a new luxury lawn made from seed is a long process, as the grasses used are slow-growing.

● Careful site preparation before seeding or turfing is all-important. Small bumps and hollows, which could well be invisible in a utility lawn, are an eyesore in the closely-shorn luxury lawn.

LUXURY LAWN GRASSES

Bents

BROWNTOP · *Agrostis tenuis*

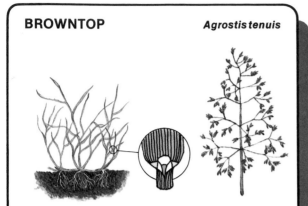

Use in lawns
The commonest of all Bents — it is present to some extent in practically all British lawns. One of the basic ingredients of luxury grass seed mixtures.

Description
A tufted grass with short stolons or rhizomes. Slow to establish, but with regular mowing forms a neat and dense turf which blends with other lawn grasses. Tough with good drought-resisting properties.

Leaves
Finely ribbed, short and tapering to a fine point.

Soil preference
Grows in all soils — well suited to dry and acid soils where it may become dominant.

BROWN BENT · *Agrostis canina montana*

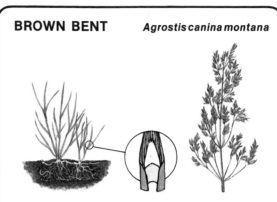

Use in lawns
Occurs in lawns in sandy and hilly areas as a native inhabitant — it does not have the quality of the modern strains of Browntop. It is not used in commercial seed mixtures.

Description
A densely tufted grass with creeping rhizomes. Slow to establish, but with regular mowing forms a neat and dense turf. High drought resistance is its outstanding property.

Leaves
Upper surface is rough to the touch. Finer than Browntop — sometimes bristle-like.

Soil preference
Grows in all soils — favourite habitat is sandy and peaty soils in upland areas.

CREEPING BENT · *Agrostis stolonifera*

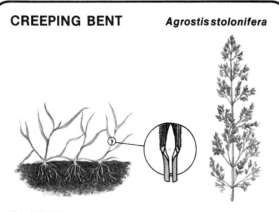

Use in lawns
Occurs in many lawns; it is one of the constituents of Cumberland turf. Occasionally used in seed mixtures, especially for chalky soils, but it is not popular. Some years ago it was available as sprigs for planting-up a new lawn.

Description
A tufted grass which spreads quickly by means of creeping stolons. With regular mowing it forms a dense turf, but it is shallow-rooted. This means that resistance to drought and hard wear is poor.

Leaves
Short and finely pointed; upper surface is smooth.

Soil preference
Favours fertile and non-acid soils.

VELVET BENT · *Agrostis canina canina*

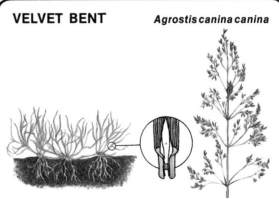

Use in lawns
Occurs in many lawns. Despite the fine leaves, it is not popular in seed mixtures — it can be distinctly disappointing in sandy soils.

Description
A tufted grass which spreads by means of creeping stolons; rather similar to Creeping Bent. Turf tends to tear during mowing and in dry soils there is an accumulation of dead fibre.

Leaves
Soft (not stiff like Brown Bent). Finer than Browntop and Creeping Bent. Look for the tell-tale long and tapering ligule.

Soil preference
Favours damp situations. Reasonably successful in shade.

Fescues

CHEWINGS FESCUE
Festuca rubra commutata

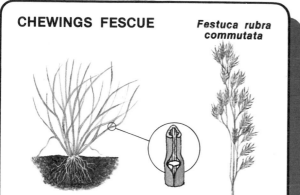

Use in lawns
One of the basic ingredients of luxury lawn seed mixtures. Blends well with other grasses, but tends to be pushed out by the more aggressive varieties.

Description
A densely tufted grass which does not produce rhizomes. It is quicker to establish than Browntop (its usual partner in high-quality seed mixtures) but it is less persistent. Tolerates close mowing but tips tend to discolour after cutting. Good drought resistance.

Leaves
Stiff and bristle-like, with a leaf sheath which is tubular — not open like Sheep's Fescue and Hard Fescue.

Soil preference
Grows in all soils, apart from heavy clays. Will succeed in dry areas.

CREEPING RED FESCUE
Festuca rubra rubra

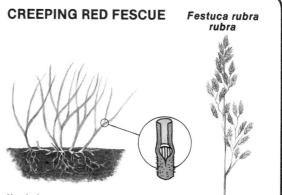

Use in lawns
Widely used in seed mixtures for the production of luxury lawns and sports turf. Growth is rather lax so it must be mixed with other varieties for the production of dense and compact turf.

Description
A creeping grass which produces slender rhizomes. Small tufts are formed at intervals, and the plants are capable of withstanding drought and cold weather. It will not tolerate very close mowing.

Leaves
Bristle-like, with sheaths which are tubular — not open like Sheep's Fescue and Hard Fescue.

Soil preference
Grows in all soils, apart from heavy clays. Prefers sandy soil.

SHEEP'S FESCUE
Festuca ovina

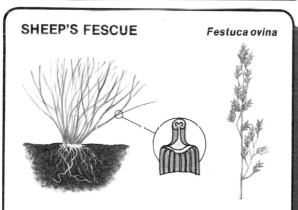

Use in lawns
Sheep's Fescue seed is scarce. It is the variety known as Fine-leaved Sheep's Fescue which is occasionally used in luxury lawn seed mixtures as a less expensive substitute for Chewings Fescue.

Description
A densely tufted grass which does not produce rhizomes. It tends to form distinct hummocks, so it does not blend well with other grasses. Withstands close mowing and dry conditions remarkably well.

Leaves
Stiff and bristle-like, the finest of all the Fescues. The leaf sheath is open — not tubular like Chewings Fescue.

Soil preference
Grows in all soils, apart from heavy clays. Will succeed in dry soils.

HARD FESCUE
Festuca longifolia

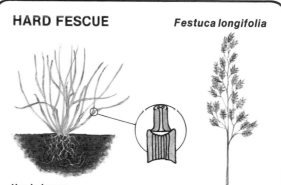

Use in lawns
Usually sold as '*Festuca duriuscula*' — an inexpensive substitute for Chewings Fescue. It is occasionally used in mixtures for lawns but it is more popular for sports turf mixtures where its low-growing habit and drought resistance are important.

Description
A densely tufted grass which does not produce rhizomes. Blends well with other grasses and withstands dry conditions remarkably well, but it is slow to establish. Withstands close mowing.

Leaves
Basal leaves are bristle-like, but stem leaves are broader. The leaf sheath is open — not tubular like Chewings Fescue.

Soil preference
Grows in all soils, apart from heavy clays. Will succeed in dry soils.

Luxury Lawns Illustrated

Luxury varieties of grasses dominate
this Scottish lawn. Some skill and
perhaps occasional re-seeding are
necessary to maintain the velvet look
in the shaded areas. ▷

◁ A narrow strip of luxury turf is of course much
easier to maintain than the large expanse
above, but the problem here is that regular
foot traffic would lead to deterioration.

△ A fine luxury lawn in a fine setting. The striped effect has
nothing to do with quality or good health — it is a feature of the
mowing technique.

THE FIRST RATE LAWN:
Utility Grade

A lawn in which Perennial Ryegrass and broad-leaved turf grasses are dominant cannot compare in beauty with a well-kept luxury lawn composed entirely of Bents and Fescues. However, if you want a lawn which is for living on rather than just looking at then the utility grade of turf is the type for you.

The first rate utility lawn will stand up to tricycles, games, washday and all the other aspects of the lawn which is used as an outdoor living area. This is an important advantage, but not the only one — the utility lawn is able to withstand moderate neglect and some bad management without serious deterioration. Poor-quality mowing which might make this grade of turf look unsightly could well result in large areas stripped bare in a luxury lawn. Most of the native coarse grasses which invade lawns are hidden in this type of turf — in the luxury lawn they would stand out as weeds. Additional advantages are the low cost of seed or turf and the ease with which the grass establishes itself in the new lawn.

There are, of course, disadvantages. The grass grows quickly in late spring and throughout the summer, so frequent cutting is essential. Also the velvet look is missing, but this can be compensated for to some extent by using a good-quality cylinder mower to impart a striped effect. This alternation of dark and light stripes in good-quality grass gives a distinctly de-luxe appearance.

The first rate utility lawn is made up of thick, closely-knit turf in which there are some Bents or Fescues amongst the coarser lawn grasses. The most popular of these lawn grasses are described on pages 16–17, and there is little disagreement amongst the experts over the relative merits of most of them.

Perennial Ryegrass aroused controversy in the past. Some felt that it should not be included in seed mixtures, but now that finer-leaved and slower-growing strains have appeared it is agreed that it has a very useful role to play.

UTILITY LAWN GRASSES

Meadow grasses

SMOOTH-STALKED MEADOW GRASS
Poa pratensis

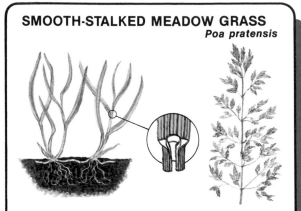

Use in lawns
The best of the Meadow grasses for turf production. A popular ingredient of seed mixtures for utility lawns — especially useful for light soils and shady sites.

Description
A creeping grass which produces slender rhizomes. Rather slow to establish, but when mature it spreads rapidly and the turf it produces is hard-wearing and resistant to dry weather. It will not tolerate frequent close mowing.

Leaves
Smooth, green or greyish-green, with smooth leaf sheaths.

Soil preference
Succeeds in a wide range of soils, except wet and chalky sites. Thrives in sandy and gravelly land.

ROUGH-STALKED MEADOW GRASS
Poa trivialis

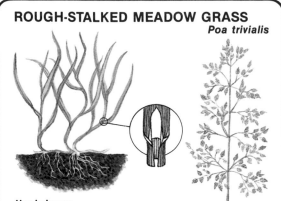

Use in lawns
An ingredient of seed mixtures for utility lawns. Useful for wet and shady sites, but generally inferior to Smooth-stalked Meadow grass — turns reddish in dry weather and surface runners are often torn by mowing.

Description
A tufted grass which spreads by means of short creeping stolons. Quicker to establish than Smooth-stalked Meadow grass, but it is less hardy, much less hard-wearing and much more susceptible to drought.

Leaves
Smooth, green or purplish-green, with rough leaf sheaths.

Soil preference
Succeeds in loamy and heavy soils, but grows best in rich moist sites.

WOOD MEADOW GRASS   *Poa nemoralis*

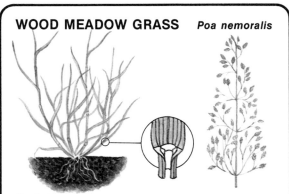

Use in lawns
A popular ingredient of mixtures which are to be sown under trees or in other shady sites. Unfortunately it cannot thrive when cut frequently so it is only suitable for areas where little or no mowing will take place.

Description
A tufted grass which does not produce rhizomes. It blends well with other grasses and it can survive deep shade, but with regular mowing it generally deteriorates and disappears.

Leaves
Soft and rich green, with smooth leaf sheaths. The leaf blades are as narrow as some luxury grasses.

Soil preference
Unlike nearly all other lawn grasses, it can thrive under shade and damp conditions.

ANNUAL MEADOW GRASS   *Poa annua*

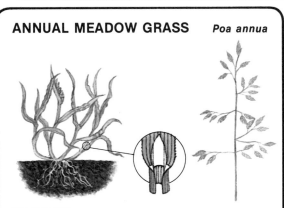

Use in lawns
Found in nearly all lawns, where it occurs naturally and spreads by seed. It is useful in many utility lawns, especially in difficult situations such as under trees, but it is a weed in luxury turf.

Description
A tufted grass, sometimes with short stolons. It sets seed nearly all year round — large areas of compacted bare patches can be quickly colonised. Withstands close mowing, but under dry conditions it turns yellow and may die.

Leaves
Soft, often crinkled when young. Smooth leaf sheaths.

Soil preference
Grows in all soil types.

Ryegrass, Timothy & Crested Dog's-tail

PERENNIAL RYEGRASS *Lolium perenne*

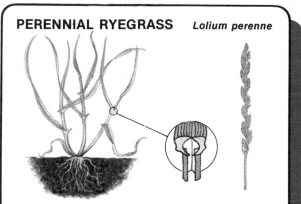

Use in lawns
An ingredient of most utility lawn seed mixtures. Hard-wearing, tolerant of heavy soils and quick to establish, it has nevertheless been long regarded as an inferior grass. The faults include growing too quickly and dying out with close mowing. Now there are excellent new varieties.

Description
Tufted grass with basal leaf sheaths which are pinkish when young. The modern varieties, such as Manhattan and Hunter, are finer-leaved, slower-growing and more tolerant of close mowing than standard Perennial Ryegrass.

Leaves
Smooth, green or dark green. Distinct 'ears' at the base of the leaf blades.

Soil preference
All soil types — thrives best in moist fertile land.

CRESTED DOG'S-TAIL *Cynosurus cristatus*

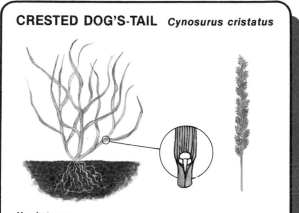

Use in lawns
An ingredient of many seed mixtures sold for utility lawns. It has its supporters as a luxury lawn grass but it does not really blend with Bents and Fescues — it also produces hard stalks which resist mowing.

Description
A tufted grass which is similar in appearance to Perennial Ryegrass, but there are no 'ears' at the base of the leaf blades and the leaf sheaths are not pink. Slow to develop, but the turf is extremely hard-wearing and resistant to dry conditions.

Leaves
Dark green, quite narrow and finely tapered at the tip.

Soil preference
Suitable for most soil types including heavy chalky land.

TIMOTHY *Phleum pratense*

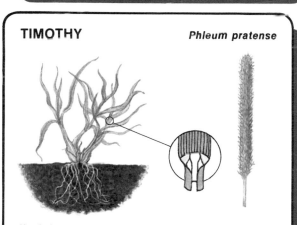

Use in lawns
An ingredient of seed mixtures for utility lawns to be grown on heavy soils. Completely unsuitable for luxury lawns — the leaves are broad and the plants cannot survive very close mowing. The recommended variety is S.48.

Description
A tufted grass with swollen stem bases. The seeds germinate quickly and a hard-wearing turf is produced which stays green even in the coldest winters.

Leaves
Rough, green or greyish-green. The leaf blades are broad but finely tapered at the tip.

Soil preference
Succeeds in heavy wet soils. It is shallow rooting and is not suitable for thin dry land.

LESSER TIMOTHY *Phleum bertolonii*

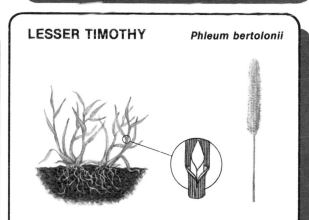

Use in lawns
An ingredient of seed mixtures for utility lawns to be grown on heavy soils. Generally better than Timothy — the leaves are finer and it will withstand closer mowing. Combines well with Bents and Fescues. The recommended variety is S.50.

Description
A tufted grass which sometimes produces leafy stolons. Stem bases are swollen. The turf is hard-wearing and capable of withstanding very cold winters.

Leaves
Smooth, green or greyish-green. The leaf blades are quite narrow, finely tapered at the tip.

Soil preference
Succeeds in heavy wet soils.

Utility Lawns Illustrated

Hard-wearing grass types such as Perennial Ryegrass are an essential feature of turf which is subjected to heavy foot traffic. Examples are a play area or the tennis court illustrated here. ▷

◁ When the lawn is large there is a considerable saving in the time required to keep it in good condition compared with the maintenance requirement of a luxury lawn.

△ When the lawn is small as in this back garden the utility grasses are able to withstand the dual problems of shade and regular traffic much better than the luxury types.

THE SECOND RATE LAWN

The vast majority of the lawns in this country are second rate. One or more of the common troubles illustrated on page 47 are present, but there is still a reasonable covering of desirable turf grasses. Your first task must be to discover the cause of the second rate condition. In this way you will be able to apply the correct cure and also know how to avoid its return once the lawn has been restored to the first rate condition.

- When making a new lawn, careful attention must be paid to site preparation, drainage and the selection of turf or seed. Carelessness at this stage is likely to result in a second rate lawn.

- Neglect is the commonest cause of the second rate condition. Neglected mowing means cutting the grass when it is overgrown and looking untidy. Over-close mowing at irregular intervals is a frequent cause of lawn deterioration. Failure to feed, water or weed are additional causes of lawn decline.

- Too much of the wrong treatment can be as harmful as too little of the right one. Liming when it isn't necessary, over-feeding in autumn and frequent use of a heavy roller can all ruin good grass.

- Many serious problems are not linked with either the ignorance or the laziness of the lawn owner. Examples are heavy shade, pests and diseases, bitch urine, heavy traffic and the drip from overhanging trees.

The second rate lawn can be generally brought back into first rate condition because the essential ingredient, a good distribution of turf grasses, is still present. Once you have discovered the cause, apply the remedy. This may be a simple treatment in the case of a single problem or it may call for a full renovation programme (see page 87) if the whole area shows serious deterioration. A second rate luxury lawn can often be greatly improved by overseeding the grass with a good quality Perennial Ryegrass-based mixture (page 96) and thereby turning it into a utility lawn.

THE WORN OUT LAWN

This type of lawn is easily distinguished from the other grades described in this chapter — you will no doubt have seen many examples in parks, paths and if you are unfortunate enough, in your own garden.

The basic feature of the worn out lawn is the absence of the desirable grasses described on pages 12–13 and 16–17. There may be a sparse covering, isolated patches or just none at all. The place of the lawn grasses has been taken by moss, coarse grass, broad-leaved weeds or bare earth. In nearly all cases the effect is extremely unsightly, but there is the special case of the green and superficially acceptable lawn which on close inspection is found to be made up entirely of pearlwort and moss.

If the whole area is in this worn out condition and you want a proper lawn, then the only thing you can do is to clear the site and start again, following the rules for the creation of a new lawn as outlined in Chapter 7.

In many cases it is only part and not the whole of the lawn which is in this condition. If only a small patch is affected, clear away the top growth and use the reclamation technique prescribed for bare patches — see page 83. If the worn out area is large and you wish to avoid creating an extensive bare patch, you can try the technique of applying Lawn Sand in late spring, raking out all the dead moss and weeds about 3 weeks later and then re-seeding the area at about 1 oz per sq. yard. Use a seed mixture which contains the grasses in the surrounding area of the lawn — use the pictures on pages 12–13 and 16–17 to identify the varieties present. The only exception is a worn out area under a tree — re-seed with a mixture which is specifically for shady sites.

Remaking or repatching the worn out lawn is only part of the answer. The original deterioration must have occurred for some reason and you should find out this cause *before* repair. The cure should then be applied before, during or after reclamation, as appropriate.

CHAPTER 3

LAWN CARE

Everybody wants a lawn to be proud of, and we all see splendid examples on our travels. The area of rich green turf may be as small as a living-room carpet or as large as the vast rolling acres surrounding a stately home, but in each case our question is always the same — "Why can't *my* lawn look like that?"

The types of grasses present in the lawn are one of the factors controlling its appearance, but the basic cause of disappointment is the lack of proper maintenance. In millions of gardens throughout Britain there are lawns which are eyesores because their owners completely misunderstand the basic principle of lawn care.

The turf is mown fairly regularly (except when we are on holiday) and the edges are kept neatly trimmed (especially when relatives are coming to stay). Apart from this routine the lawn is expected to look after itself, except when trouble strikes. When the grass looks pale we buy a fertilizer, and when it turns brown after weeks without rain we rush out and water. Moss and weeds appear, and when the patches become large enough to disfigure the surface we rush out and buy a bottle of something to eradicate the problem. In short, we wait for signs of neglect to appear and then, if we are garden-proud, we try to cure them.

A lawn needs better treatment than that if it is to be a thing of beauty. The basic principle of lawn care is to carry out a number of straight-forward routine tasks which are designed to keep the grass vigorous as well as attractive, which means that troubles are kept at bay. Thus a proper maintenance programme is a series of trouble-preventing measures and not a series of emergency treatments.

Unfortunately, the list of jobs set out in the text books (including this one!) is quite frightening. You *should* top dress the lawn every autumn, you *should* always brush the wet grass before mowing, you *should* spike the compacted lawn at regular intervals ... but for most people this counsel of perfection by the experts is just not possible. It's fine if the lawn is your hobby and you have plenty of time, otherwise you must settle for a routine which is half-way between the partial neglect by the average gardener and the complete programme practised by the perfectionist.

On the next page is a list of jobs you *must* do during the year if you want a lawn which will not be a constant problem; on page 24 you will find details of the equipment required for these tasks. A number of tools and several jobs are listed as essential, but buying a good mower and learning to mow properly are the paramount needs. Make a mistake here and all is lost, for no amount of feeding, top dressing, weeding and so on can make up for the damage caused. Forget the advertisements which show how one mower will produce a superb bowling green whereas another will make you weep with shame. The great need is for a mower with sufficient power to cope with the turf area involved and with blades which are sharp and properly set. Then you must use it frequently and regularly to cut the grass to the correct height. Research has shown that close cropping is one of the quickest ways to spoil the home lawn. On page 31 you will find detailed instructions, but a useful rule-of-thumb is once a week to leave the grass ¾ to 1 inch high.

On page 23 is a list of those extra jobs for the gardener who wants a lawn which will make people say — "Why can't *my* lawn look like that?"

LAWN CARE | THE JOBS YOU HAVE TO DO

THE ESSENTIAL TASKS

The immediate effect of the essential tasks such as mowing, watering, feeding and weeding is to keep the lawn looking attractive, but there is also a vital long-term effect. The vigour of the desirable grasses is maintained and increased so that unwelcome invaders such as weeds, moss and some diseases find it harder to gain a foothold.

Feed with a nitrogen-rich fertilizer in spring or early summer

The constant cropping of the grass foliage is a serious drain on the nutrient reserves in the soil, so a routine feed is essential at the early part of the growing season. It is nonsense to refrain from feeding because it will mean more mowing — starvation results in thin and sparse grass.

Mow regularly

The number one essential task is correct mowing. This means beginning and ending at the proper time (see page 31) with the blades set at the correct height. There is no 'right' height for all lawns. This will depend on the type of lawn and the time of the year — see page 31. The blades must be sharp and properly set.

Rake during the spring and again in the autumn

Raking the lawn with a spring-tine rake has several benefits. The build-up of thatch (page 43) is prevented, and surface debris is removed.

The removal of fallen leaves in autumn is essential — never leave them on the surface over winter. Raking up creeping stems of weeds before mowing helps in their control. Wheeled rakes are now available.

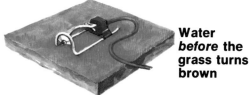

Water *before* the grass turns brown

The first effect of drought in lawns is a loss of springiness and a general dullness of the turf. Look for these signs after about 7 days of dry weather in summer or 10 days in spring. Then water copiously as recommended on page 38 — note that a light sprinkling every day can do more harm than good.

Remove worm casts when they appear

Worm casts should never be ignored. When squashed underfoot the surface is rendered uneven and the bare earth makes an ideal seed bed for weeds. When casts appear scatter them with a besom before mowing and removing the clippings by using a grass box. Using Lawn Sand helps to control worms.

Trim the edges

A lawn with overgrown grass at the edges can be an eyesore. Make sure that the mower can reach right up to the edge — see the notes on good design on pages 8–9. Then trim around the edges after mowing with one of the many pieces of equipment available for this job (see page 40). Make sure that the edge trimmer is sharp.

Kill weeds and moss when they appear

Don't wait until the problems get out of hand. Occasional weeds can be pulled out — occasional patches of moss indicate that the growing conditions have to be improved. Apply a weedkiller or moss killer promptly as soon as there is an obvious invasion. No single product can do everything — use the right chemical or non-chemical technique by reading the Weeds section (pages 52–79).

ADDITIONAL TASKS FOR THE SHOWPIECE LAWN

Aerate the lawn

The lawn is aerated by driving in a fork or other spiked instrument at intervals so as to relieve compaction — drainage is improved and new growth is stimulated. Aerate at least once a year if the ground is badly compacted and moss is present. It should be sufficient to aerate once every 3 years if a hollow-tine fork is used for spiking.

Brush the surface regularly

The skilled gardener regards the besom or birch broom as an important piece of lawn equipment. Surface dew or raindrops should always be swished away before mowing, and worm casts must be dispersed before the mower is used. Even when dew and worm casts are absent, the professional green-keeper will still brush his turf before mowing.

Top dress the lawn

Top dressing is the application of a bulky mixture, usually made up of peat, loam and sand. This dressing should be applied every autumn, and it is an essential technique if you want a really first rate lawn. There are many benefits, as described on page 35 — the vigour of grass is improved and minor hollows are removed.

Apply routine treatments for moss, weeds and disease

Most lawn problems are extremely difficult to control once they have become established. Many keen lawn owners therefore follow a preventative programme by using Lawn Sand every spring for moss control, a selective weedkiller in late spring and a disease preventative each autumn.

Feed with a balanced fertilizer in autumn

Autumn feeding to build up the root system and increase disease resistance is a useful procedure, but you must choose your fertilizer with care. The nitrogen rich feeds of spring and summer are not suitable — they can stimulate soft growth and increase the risk of disease. Pick a product which clearly states that it is for autumn use.

Tackle brown patches as soon as they appear

The average gardener will try to do something about a brown patch when it has enlarged to become an eyesore. This will not do for the showpiece lawn — brown patches should be carefully examined and control measures taken while they are still small and have not yet reached the unsightly stage. The causes of brown patches are many and varied — see pages 80–81.

OTHER TASKS — BUT ONLY IF NECESSARY

Roll — but only if necessary

In the hands of the skilled professional greenkeeper the roller plays a useful part in lawn maintenance. In the hands of the unskilled gardener it will do much more harm than good. The only time to roll is in spring when the surface is dry and the soil is damp. See page 46 for more details. Remember the rule — if in doubt, don't roll.

Apply lime — but only if necessary

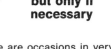

Lime is rarely needed. There are occasions in very acid soil when a light dressing of limestone is beneficial, but adding lime to a lawn which does not need it can lead to serious deterioration of the turf. See page 46 for more details. Remember the rule — if in doubt, don't lime.

LAWN CARE   THE EQUIPMENT YOU WILL NEED

THE ESSENTIAL TOOLS

MOWER

The most important item. Despite all the aggressive advertising, there is no one mower which is ideal for all lawns. The correct choice depends on the size of your lawn and the depth of your pocket. Pages 26–30 should help you to pick wisely.

SPRING-TINE RAKE

Essential for cleaning up the lawn surface in the spring and for the removal of leaves and other debris in autumn. This treatment has a tonic effect by preventing the build-up of thatch.

LONG-HANDLED EDGING SHEARS

Essential for trimming the edges after mowing. Ordinary hand shears make this a back-breaking job unless the lawn is very small. For the larger than average lawn there are many different sorts of mechanical edger.

GARDEN FORK

The simplest way to aerate the turf deeply enough to relieve compaction.

HOSE & SPRINKLER

The effect of drought is more serious than just unsightly browning — the weakened grass is susceptible to weed and moss invasion once the rain returns. Copious watering is essential in a dry summer, so an efficient sprinkler is necessary.

BESOM

Brushing is necessary for a variety of jobs — see page 42. A besom or birch broom is usually considered more suitable than a stiff yard brush. There is no need to buy an expensive broom, but do replace it when the bristles are worn.

WATERING CAN

Too small for watering, but very useful for the application of weedkillers, moss killers and liquid feeds.

STRAIGHT PLANK

A large plank (8–10 ft long) is essential for checking on the presence of bumps and hollows in the lawn. It is also used when cutting the edge of a square or rectangular lawn with a half-moon edging iron.

SMALL TROWEL OR HANDFORK

Isolated rosette weeds can be dug out of the turf — trying to pull them out by the leaves usually results in the roots being left behind.

LOOK AFTER YOURSELF

Each year when the mowing season starts there is an increase in the number of out-patients at our hospitals. The situation has got worse with the increase in popularity of power mowers, and you must follow the common-sense rules if you are not to become an accident statistic. Always disconnect the power supply before making any adjustments. Mowers aren't the only source of trouble — never leave a garden rake with its teeth uppermost on the lawn and never thrust a garden fork downwards until you have checked that your feet are well clear. When using chemicals read the precautions before you begin. Protect your eyes when using a nylon cord trimmer.

ADDITIONAL TOOLS

FERTILIZER SPREADER
If you have a large area of lawn to cover this tool is essential for the even distribution of powder or granular lawn dressings.

LIGHT ROLLER
For use in the spring after frost — not a necessary piece of equipment unless you have a mower without a back roller.

HALF-MOON EDGING IRON
Useful for obtaining a neat edge at the start of the season, but it must not be used too often.

SIEVE
Choose one with ¼ in. mesh. Necessary for the preparation of top dressings.

HOLLOW-TINE FORK
Useful for the deep aeration of the turf to improve the drainage in heavy soil.

SOLID-TINE AERATOR
Useful for the shallow aeration of the turf to improve the penetration of air and water into the topsoil. Effect on deeper compaction is slight.

MECHANICAL SWEEPER
Wheeled brush which saves a lot of time on the large lawn in autumn. Vacuum blowers and collectors are available.

EDGING
A metal or plastic aid to stop grass spreading into flower beds and to keep the edges firm.

SLITTER AERATOR
Useful for the shallow aeration of the turf to improve the penetration of air and water into the topsoil. Effect on deeper compaction is usually slight unless the machine is heavy.

MECHANICAL RAKE
A useful double-purpose tool — it will pick up clippings and other surface debris after mowing and will also sweep up leaves in autumn.

HOSE END DILUTOR
Useful for the application of liquid lawn foods or moss killers over large areas.

MECHANICAL EDGER
A hand-powered or electrically driven trimmer which cuts vertically. Many gardeners find the mechanical edger no quicker or easier to use than long-handled shears.

MECHANICAL TRIMMER
A power-driven trimmer which cuts horizontally. Useful for cutting grass around trees or walls — the nylon cord trimmer is light and easy to use.

LOOK AFTER YOUR TOOLS
Lawn tools have to be kept sharp and rust-free, otherwise they are inefficient and early replacement may be necessary. After use, remove caked grass and earth from all equipment — use a stiff brush if necessary. Removal of mud is simple at this stage — later on it may have to be scraped off. When clean, dry off any surface moisture and then wipe with an oily rag. Winter storage is the danger time for corrosion. Make sure that the storage facilities are reasonable — all tools should be cleaned and oiled according to the maker's instructions. Corrosion-inhibiting aerosols are available and are worth considering.

LAWN CARE MOWING

"Country gentlemen will find in using my machine an amusing, useful and healthful exercise . . ."
Original cylinder mower patent issued to Edwin Budding 1830.

Once there were only hand mowers, but ever since 1900 the well-to-do gardener with a large lawn has been able to buy a labour-saving alternative — the petrol-driven cylinder mower. During the 1970s the lightweight electric mower steadily took over from both of them and by 1975 half the mowers being sold were motor-driven. Today the figure has risen to more than 90 per cent.

The term 'motor-driven' can be misleading. In most cases the power is used to drive the blades and not the wheels — it is only the more expensive cylinder and rotary models which are self-propelled.

There are hundreds of different models in all shapes and sizes from which to make your choice, and despite the advertising there is no 'right' machine for every situation. The best machine for your lawn is one which is large enough to tackle the job quickly and comfortably but small enough to fit in with your budget.

If you want a new mower, choose the power source from the chart below. Next study the types of machine available and finally answer the questions on page 30. You should then be in a position to go along to your supplier and make a wise choice.

TYPES OF POWER

It used to be simply a matter of buying a hand mower if the lawn was small and money was limited — a motor mower was for people with more turf and more money. Now things are quite different — a light electric mower costs less than a good quality hand-driven machine.

HAND-DRIVEN

Once all mowers were hand-driven, now more than 90 per cent of all the models sold are motorised. For a small lawn there are still advantages — nothing to go wrong, no fuel bills, no noise and perhaps the finest cut of all if a high-quality cylinder model is used. But pushing can be a chore, especially if the grass is damp or overgrown.

ELECTRIC-DRIVEN

Electric models dominate the market — more than 4 out of every 5 mowers now sold work from the mains. It is the lightweight versions which have led to this popularity — they are inexpensive and efficient for the smaller lawn. There are many advantages compared with the petrol-driven mower — they are quieter and easier to maintain. But about 200 ft of flex is the maximum — for large areas of grass a petrol model should be considered.

BATTERY-DRIVEN

Once battery-driven mowers were popular — they combined the quietness and lightness of the electric mower with the cable-free advantage of the petrol-driven model. Despite these advantages, not many models are available.

PETROL-DRIVEN

A petrol-driven model is both heavier and dearer than an electric model with the same cutting width, but it has more power and also the great advantage of being independent of an external power source. The tiresome job of moving the cable and the fear of cutting through it are avoided.

TYPES OF MOWER

RIDE-ON MOWERS

WALK-BEHIND MOWERS

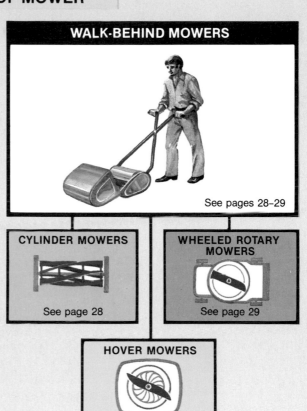

See pages 28–29

CYLINDER MOWERS

See page 28

WHEELED ROTARY MOWERS

See page 29

HOVER MOWERS

See page 29

A WORD OF WARNING

Mains electricity is the most popular source of power and unfortunately this results in many serious accidents every year. If you buy an electric model do read the instructions carefully before use. Leads and connectors must be outdoor quality and check regularly for loose connections. Above all have a circuit breaker to cut off the current if the machine becomes live — Residual Current Device (RCD) plugs are available.

RIDE-ON MOWERS

There are now many different types available for the large lawn — about half an acre makes this type worthwhile but by no means essential. The most popular version is the four-wheeled tractor bearing a rotary cutter.

Advantages
Cuts large areas quickly. Most people find it enjoyable to use, as the chore of walking behind the machine is removed. Regarded by many as a status-symbol!

Disadvantages
Expensive, and difficult to use in awkward corners. Wide and level passageway essential between garage and lawn. Compaction of heavy wet land can be a problem.

TRAILING SEAT MOWER

TRACTOR MOWER

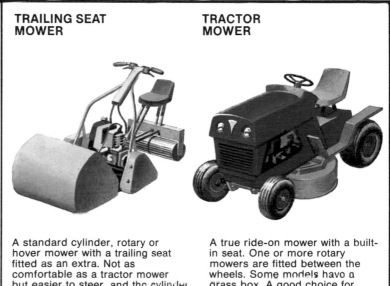

A standard cylinder, rotary or hover mower with a trailing seat fitted as an extra. Not as comfortable as a tractor mower but easier to steer, and the cylinder version gives a better finish.
Cutting widths available: 21–30 in.

A true ride-on mower with a built-in seat. One or more rotary mowers are fitted between the wheels. Some models have a grass box. A good choice for large areas of rough grass.
Cutting widths available: 24–44 in.

TYPES OF MOWER continued

WALK-BEHIND MOWERS

CYLINDER MOWERS
Cut with a scissor-like action

The grass is cut between a series of moving blades and a bottom fixed blade. The moving blades are arranged spirally around a central shaft, and their number and speed of rotation determine the fineness of the cut.

5–6 blades are the standard, but 8–12 are needed to give a bowling green effect. These multi-blade machines are expensive.

3 blade machines have become very popular. The cylinder rotates at high speed and grass several inches high can be tackled — an unusual feature for a cylinder mower.

Advantages
The cylinder mower gives the best and cleanest cut of all mower types. It can be set to cut more closely than the others, and is the type to choose for a luxury lawn.

Disadvantages
Robust cylinder mowers are expensive compared with their rotary or hover equivalents. Careful setting of the blades is essential, and all cylinder mowers with more than 3 blades perform badly if the grass is long. Wiry grass stalks are not cut.

HAND-DRIVEN ROLLER MOWER

An excellent choice for a small plot with flower beds and awkward corners. The back roller gives a good finish to the cut turf, and grass collection by the front-mounted box is usually very good. It is less inclined to scalp the lawn than a sidewheel mower, and it can of course be used along the lawn edge.
Cutting widths available: 10–16 in.

HAND-DRIVEN SIDEWHEEL MOWER

The simplest and cheapest of all mowers. It is superior to a roller mower for new lawns or overgrown turf, but it has the serious disadvantage that it cannot be used right up to the edge of the lawn. The grass box is often back-mounted and grass collection is sometimes disappointing.
Cutting widths available: 12–14 in.

ELECTRIC-DRIVEN CYLINDER MOWER

The lightweight 12 in. model has become popular — it is a good choice for a small or average-size patch of ornamental lawn, but it is not designed for heavy work or large lawns.

For large plots self-propelled versions are available. All electrics, big and small, are quieter, cheaper and easier to manoeuvre than their petrol counterparts, but they are less powerful.
Cutting widths available: 12–14 in.

PETROL-DRIVEN CYLINDER MOWER

The correct choice for an extensive stretch of luxury lawn. A wide cutting width can be chosen, and there is maximum power. Drawbacks outnumber the advantages for an average-sized lawn. The machines are heavy, noisy and maintenance costs higher than for the electrical equivalent, so petrol-driven cylinder mowers are not the popular choice.
Cutting widths available: 12–42 in.

TYPES OF MOWER continued

WHEELED ROTARY MOWERS
Cut with a scythe-like action

The grass is cut by a blade or group of blades rotating horizontally at high speed. Wheels or wheels-plus-roller support the machine above the lawn.

Advantages
The rotary mower is an excellent general-purpose tool. It will give an acceptable cut on the front lawn and also deal effectively with rough turf and overgrown grass. Blade adjustment is easy, and large models are cheaper than cylinder equivalents.

Disadvantages
The quality of the cut is not as good as that obtained with a properly-set cylinder mower. Small models have no grass collection facility.

ELECTRIC-DRIVEN ROTARY MOWER

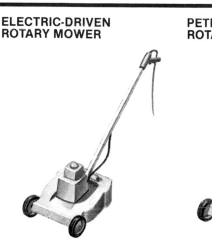

The lightweight 12 in. model has become popular and is a good all-purpose machine for the utility lawn. It is not designed to tackle long wet grass where more power is needed, and the inexpensive smaller models do not roll the turf nor pick up the clippings. At the top end of the market there are self-propelled models with grass collectors and back rollers.
Cutting widths available: 10–18 in.

PETROL-DRIVEN ROTARY MOWER

For large areas of utility lawn a petrol-driven rotary mower is a good choice. If the width of cut is wide you should consider a self-propelled model, as pushing a heavy machine over the lawn can be very tiring. A rear-mounted grass box is usually present. Some have a vacuum action, sucking the clippings into the box.
Cutting widths available; 14–30 in.

HOVER MOWERS
Cut with a scythe-like action

The grass is cut by a blade rotating horizontally at high speed. A fan beneath the canopy builds up an air cushion on which the machine floats.

Advantages
The hover mower is easier to move across the lawn than the other mower types. Awkward corners are reached with ease, and mowing over wet yielding turf is no problem. Rough, bumpy turf and overgrown grass can be dealt with, and little space is needed for storage.

Disadvantages
Difficult to keep in a straight line, and dust, grass clippings etc. are thrown about when in use. Extra care is needed to avoid accidents when using the machine.

ELECTRIC-DRIVEN HOVER MOWER

The 12 in. electric hover has become popular in recent years — it is light, fast and easy to maintain. Some people like the freedom of the gliding action — others prefer the directional control given by wheels. Grass clippings are not collected by the cheaper models, and this can be a problem (see page 31).
Cutting widths available: 10–19 in.

PETROL-DRIVEN HOVER MOWER

The petrol-driven version of the hover mower is much less popular than its electric counterpart. It is heavier, noisier and more expensive, but it is free from the restriction of the cable (a hazard with hover mowers) and it will cut thick wet grass which could stall a small electric model.
Cutting widths available: 15–19 in.

CHOOSING A MOWER

How much lawn do I have?

This used to be the basic question for deciding whether to invest in a motorised mower. It is no longer a controlling factor — light electric mowers are now as cheap or cheaper than hand-driven models. If you are fit and enjoy the exercise, a lawn up to 700 sq. ft can be quite easily tackled with a hand mower — beyond that an electric- or petrol-driven mower is a good idea.

How quickly do I want to cut the lawn?

Hover mowers will generally cut a lawn more quickly than either a cylinder or rotary model, but the real deciding factor is the width of cut. It will take you about 12 minutes to cut 1000 sq. ft of grass with a 12 in. petrol-driven cylinder mower — increase the cutting width to 14 in. and the time goes down to 10½ minutes. The mower to buy is a compromise between the need for speed and the need for convenience and saving money. The standard width for a small lawn (up to 750 sq. ft) is 12 in. and for an average-sized lawn (750–1500 sq. ft) a 14 in. cutting width is recommended. Large lawns (1500–5000 sq. ft) need a cutting width of 16 in. at the lower end of this range and a 20 in. width at the higher end. For the very large lawn you will require a self-propelled or ride-on petrol mower with a cutting width of at least 22 in.

Is the turf bumpy or rough?

Choose a rotary or hover mower, not a cylinder model.

Do I want the best possible finish?

A cylinder mower will give you the cleanest and the closest cut — a grass box will remove the clippings. A back roller is essential if you want a striped look (see page 32).

Is safety a prime consideration?

Cylinder mowers are basically safer than rotary and hover models, but all mowers can be dangerous if handled carelessly.

Am I prepared to have grass clippings on the lawn?

Clippings on the lawn are unsightly, and can lead to degeneration of the turf. The front-mounted box is the most effective collection system. The back-mounted box or bag on some rotary mowers is quite effective, but tends to clog if the clippings are wet. The collection systems on larger hover mowers are not very effective.

What shape is the lawn?

If the lawn is square or rectangular, choose the largest mower you can afford, store and handle — it will save you time and make the job easier. But if there are flower beds, narrow verges and awkward corners, ease of handling is more important than size.

Is a power point available and is every part of the lawn within 200 ft of it?

If the answer is no, then forget about buying an electric-driven model. Choose a petrol-driven one or find a second-hand battery mower.

Is the grass likely to be overgrown?

Holidays can mean that the lawn is left for a fortnight or more during the growing season. A hover or rotary mower will tackle the problem easily and a petrol-driven mower is better than an electric one.

Do I need a self-propelled mower?

Most motorised mowers use the power source to drive the blades, but you have to push them across the lawn. Little effort is required with a hover mower, but with other models this can be exhausting if the area is large and the machine heavy and cumbersome. Rotary mowers with a cutting width of 20 in. or more and cylinder mowers with a cut of 16 in. or more usually require to be self-propelled. Having the mower driven along by the motor makes the job of cutting the lawn much easier, especially if the land is sloping, but it does make the mower less manoeuvrable and more expensive.

SMALL ELECTRIC HOVER   or   SMALL ELECTRIC CYLINDER

Choose it for a small or average-sized lawn, where speed and ease are all-important. Both smooth and bumpy surfaces can be mown. Neglected grass can be dealt with, but frequent mowing is necessary to stop the clippings which remain behind from being unsightly.

Choose it for a small or average-sized lawn, where a high-quality finish is all-important. The lawn surface should be smooth. Neglected grass can be dealt with, but frequent mowing is necessary to maintain the quality of the turf — a rule which applies to *all* mowers.

THE MOWING OPERATION

The purpose of mowing is not merely to keep down unsightly growth. When correctly carried out, it builds up a vigorous, fine quality grass sward. The secret is to **keep the grass long enough to prevent the roots from being starved but short enough to be attractive to the observer. This height must not vary a great deal during the growing season.**

Mowing takes more time than any other lawn operation, and trials have shown that it has a controlling influence on the make-up of the turf. The varieties of grass in a first rate lawn will dramatically change if the height of cut is either raised or lowered for a long period.

The rule is to mow often, but not too closely. In this way excess leaf-growth is prevented, fertilizer loss curtailed, and the menace of weeds, worms and coarse grasses reduced. The grass itself assumes a dwarf habit and the production of tillers is stimulated. It is the development of these side-shoots which thickens the lawn in summer.

Close shaving at irregular intervals is unfortunately an all-too-common practice. It means certain destruction of the good quality lawn because the desirable grasses are rapidly weakened. The thin open turf which results is soon invaded by moss, pearlwort, annual meadow grass, daisies and yarrow.

HEIGHT OF CUT

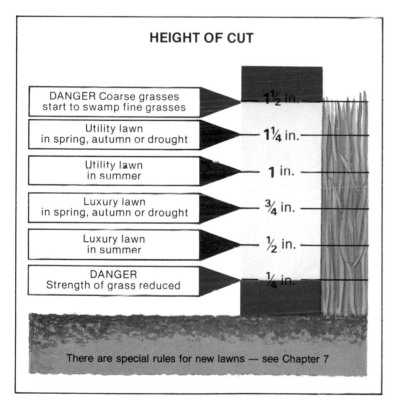

DANGER Coarse grasses start to swamp fine grasses	1½ in.
Utility lawn in spring, autumn or drought	1¼ in.
Utility lawn in summer	1 in.
Luxury lawn in spring, autumn or drought	¾ in.
Luxury lawn in summer	½ in.
DANGER Strength of grass reduced	¼ in.

There are special rules for new lawns — see Chapter 7

WHEN TO CUT

Begin in March and finish in October, apart from occasional light 'topping' in early winter when the weather is mild.

The correct frequency of cutting during the growing season will depend on many factors, such as lawn type, variety, weather, soil fertility, grass vigour and the time of the year. The height of the grass is the best guide — at cutting time it should not be more than ½ in. above the recommended height. As a rough guide —

Cut **twice a week** when the grass is growing vigorously in summer.

Cut **once a week** in spring, autumn and during prolonged dry spells in summer.

Cutting less than once a week when the grass is actively growing results in the sudden loss of a large quantity of leaf. This shocks the grass and reduces its vigour, and this results in open turf followed by the invasion of moss and weeds. If the grass has grown tall while you have been on holiday, then merely tip it at the first cut. Reduce the height at the next cut a few days later, after which you can cut at the recommended height.

USING THE GRASS BOX

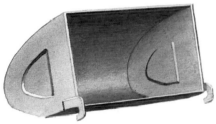

There is a temptation to leave clippings on the lawn — nutrients are returned to the soil, drought resistance is improved, moss is inhibited and you are saved the chore of taking the clippings away.

In most cases, however, the disadvantages far outweigh the advantages. Weeds are spread, the turf becomes spongy and susceptible to disease, worm activity is greatly encouraged and aeration is impeded.

The general rule is to remove grass clippings each time you mow, but if the weather is hot and dry and if the turf is reasonably weed-free, leave the clippings on the lawn to cut down water loss from the surface.

BEFORE MOWING

1 Set the blades at the correct height. Use the table on page 31 as your guide and look in the manufacturer's instruction book for the method of changing the height of cut. Make sure that *both* sides of the machine are set at the same height — a sloping cut is unsightly at best, disastrous at worst.

2 Whenever possible choose a time when the grass foliage is dry — mowing wet turf can produce a ragged effect and clog the machine. The soil beneath should also be reasonably dry — mowing waterlogged turf with a cylinder or rotary mower will damage the surface, with the roller or wheels sinking into the soft ground. Obviously, using an electric machine in soaking turf is a safety hazard.

3 Clean-up the surface. Remove sticks, stones, bones, pet droppings, wire … in fact all objects which could obviously damage the mower or form an unsightly mess under the pressure of the machine.

4 Brushing the surface after the clean-up is often a useful technique, especially if the surface is wet with dew or raindrops. Worm casts are spread about and both grass leaves and the runners of weeds are raised to meet the blades. Light raking is an alternative technique, but should only be used occasionally — see page 43.

5 Plan the direction of mowing — this should be at right angles to the previous cut. If the work has been carried out in a north-south line, then the next cutting should be in an east-west direction. This helps to keep the coarse grasses under control and also prevents washboarding (see page 86).

6 Know your machine, especially if it has been recently acquired. Know how to stop it quickly in case of emergency. Fill up with petrol *before* you start to cut the grass.

7 During late autumn or early winter never mow the lawn when a cold strong wind is blowing — the grass tips will be scorched and remain so all winter.

WHEN MOWING

1 Zebra stripes, those alternate light and dark bands seen so often on mown lawns, are taken by many people to be a sign of quality. They are nothing of the sort. These bands are the result of the lawn being cut in parallel strips with a mower fitted with a roller, the alternate stripes being mown in opposite directions as shown below. An attractive technique, especially as it helps to mask minor imperfections or colour variations, but it is unsightly if not done accurately and neatly.

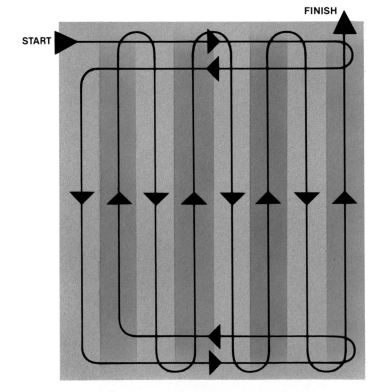

2 Use the correct technique. A mower is *not* a vacuum cleaner, and is not designed for pushing backwards and forwards as you move along. This push-pull technique is time-wasting with a cylinder mower, risky with a rotary mower and positively dangerous with a hover mower. The correct procedure is to move in a constant forward direction at a steady walking pace. The only exception is when you are manoeuvering in awkward corners.

3 Never leave the machine unattended with the engine running and the cutter blades disengaged. Switch off.

4 Electric mowers call for good cable sense. Make sure that the cable is well away from the mower when it is in use, and keep people and pets off the lawn when you are mowing.

5 Wear sensible clothing. If the area is slippery or sloping then stout shoes or boots are a good idea. Never mow in your bare feet — such advice should be unnecessary but hospital records show it isn't!

6 Despite the advertising, sloping banks are not child's play for any type of mower. The hover machine is perhaps the best model to use, but you should handle it carefully. Move the mower from side to side in a sweeping semi-circular motion.

7 When using a rotary mower fitted with a grass box, occasionally clean the grass box slots to ensure that the suction system is satisfactory. This is especially important if the grass is wet and long.

8 Never, never make any adjustments while the power is on. However small the problem, however sure and experienced you are, switch off the power before approaching the cutting mechanism.

AFTER MOWING AND MAINTENANCE

1 A quick wipe of the blades and then back into the garage or shed to await the next visit to the lawn is *not* the way to look after your mower. Proper cleaning and a careful check for faults should take place either just after mowing or in good time before the next cut. There is nothing more annoying in gardening than to have to spend an hour or two repairing or cleaning the machine before mowing, only to find that rain has started to fall just when you are ready to go on the lawn.

2 The first thing is to move the machine on to a hard surface. Disconnect the power supply. Unplug an electric mower — with a petrol mower shut off the fuel supply and then allow the engine to cut out with the drive disconnected.

3 With a rag and stiff brush remove all clippings and caked earth. The areas to be cleaned are the grass box, blades, rollers, cylinders and under the canopy of a rotary or hover mower. Dry the various parts and then wipe over with an oily rag.

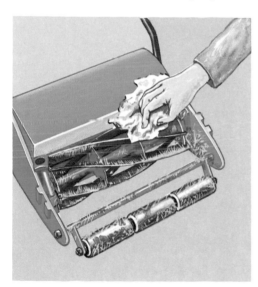

4 A battery mower should be recharged immediately after use. Every fortnight examine the water levels in the cells — top up with distilled water as necessary. Wire brush the battery terminals occasionally and coat them with petroleum jelly.

5 Check the blades. If a blade or cutter assembly has been damaged or is loose, the mower could be inefficient or positively dangerous if used again before it is repaired. With a rotary mower, check that the bolt holding the cutter bar is tight. If this cutter bar is blunt it can be sharpened quite easily with a reaper file, but if it is badly worn or damaged you should take the machine to your dealer to have a new blade fitted and balanced.

6 Re-sharpening damaged blades of a cylinder mower is not easy, but you can buy a simple tool (the Multi-sharp Cylinder Mower Sharpener) to give a keener edge to blades which are in good condition. It is clipped on to the bottom fixed blade and the cylinder rotated for a few minutes.

7 A cylinder mower with sharp blades will still cut badly if the distance between the moving blades and the fixed blade is not correct. Check the cutting action by placing a piece of paper between one of the moving blades and the bottom fixed blade. Revolve the cylinder — watch your fingers! The paper should be cut cleanly, and the same thing should happen at all points along the cutting surface. Adjust the cutting action by turning the end screws until the gap is close enough to shear the paper cleanly.

8 Running over a stone may cause a 'high spot' on the blade. This can interfere with smooth running of the cylinder and should be rubbed down with a file.

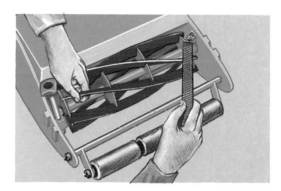

AFTER MOWING AND MAINTENANCE contd.

9 Carry out regular routine maintenance. Oil the front rollers and cutting cylinder bearings. Apply grease (not oil) to the chains and clean the air filters.

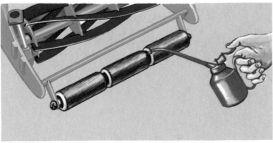

10 The remaining routine maintenance tasks will depend on the source of power. Petrol mowers should have the oil level checked. Top up if necessary; if the oil in the sump is black then change it. Look for leaks — oil and petrol dripping on to the lawn will cause scorch. An electric mower should be checked carefully to ensure that all wires and plugs are in good condition and firmly held.

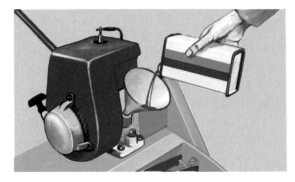

11 Correct storage is essential. The mower must be kept under cover, of course, and there should be no chance of rain or dripping water reaching it. A hover mower can be conveniently hung on the wall.

When the mower won't start

In the lifetime of every motor mower there will be an occasion when it refuses to start. Even if you know nothing about machinery there are a number of checks you can carry out.

- Is there oil and petrol in the machine?
- Has the petrol been standing for several months?
- Are all the leads connected?
- Has the fuse blown?
- Is the air filter clean?

Your detailed guide must be the manufacturer's instruction book — make sure you have a copy *before* the machine breaks down. Follow the faults chart and fix it if you can, but *don't* attempt a complex repair unless you have the necessary skills and tools. It is much better to take it to your local machinery dealer.

Getting ready for winter

PETROL MOWER
Drain off all oil and petrol. Clean and adjust the gap of each sparking plug.

Carry out general autumn maintenance (see below) and then top up with clean engine oil, as recommended by the manufacturer.

BATTERY MOWER
Remove the battery, top up with distilled water, re-charge and then store in a warm dry place.

Carry out general autumn maintenance (see below).

ELECTRIC MOWER
Check all leads for loose connections. Carefully examine the cable for cracking or physical damage. If a cut is detected, repair with a special waterproof connector — never use insulating tape. Carry out general autumn maintenance (see below).

GENERAL AUTUMN MAINTENANCE — ALL MODELS
Clean away all mud and grass — rub off any rust with wire wool or a wire brush. Oil or grease all bearings, and the exposed metal parts should be sprayed with a water-repellent anti-rust aerosol. Store the mower on wood or hardboard rather than on concrete or earth.

This programme is designed for a mower which is in good condition. If cutting has been poor or if there has been a loss of power, send the machine to a reputable service organisation. Book this service in autumn — do not wait until the grass has started to grow in the spring.

LAWN CARE TOP DRESSING

Top dressing is the application of bulky material to the surface of the turf. This material is usually a mixture of good-quality soil, sand and a source of humus. The annual application of this top dressing is a matter of routine for the professional greenkeeper, but it is an unheard-of technique for nearly all home gardeners. Its purpose is to fill in all the minor hollows which have developed during the season and to build up an ideal soil layer over the years. For a really first rate turf you should copy the professional and top dress every year.

Making up the mixture

The ingredients should be fairly dry and thorough mixing is essential before use. If the top dressing is lumpy then pass it through a ¼ in. mesh sieve.

 PEAT Buy a fine-grade sphagnum or sedge peat. Well-decomposed leaf mould is a satisfactory substitute. Garden compost is best avoided — weed seeds can be a problem.

 LOAM This is soil which is neither clayey nor sandy. The best loam is obtained from grass turves stacked grass-downwards until well-rotted and then passed through a ¼ in. mesh sieve, but any good garden soil will do.

 SAND Sea sand is not suitable as it must be lime-free. The particle size should not be too large — avoid coarse grit.

For lawns on heavy soil

For lawns on loamy soil

For lawns on sandy soil

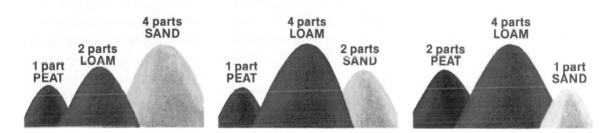

1 part PEAT · 2 parts LOAM · 4 parts SAND

1 part PEAT · 4 parts LOAM · 2 parts SAND

2 parts PEAT · 4 parts LOAM · 1 part SAND

How to apply top dressing

The best time is early autumn — mid September is ideal. Scarify the lawn if thatch is present (see page 43). Spiking a day or two before top dressing will greatly increase the benefits obtained in heavy or compacted soil.

Spread at the rate of 3 lb per sq. yard, using a spade to put down small heaps over the surface. This top dressing must be worked well into the surface so that it is knocked off the grass blades and sifted down to soil level. On no account should the grass be smothered.

A birch broom is often used, but the top dressing may be spread unevenly and so one of the main purposes of the treatment can be lost. Use instead the flat back of a wooden rake or ordinary garden rake. If you have a large area to treat, construct a home-made lute from a 5 ft plank as illustrated.

Whatever spreader is used, it is essential to spread the top dressing evenly over the surface so that depressions are filled in and no new bumps are created. After spreading, it may be necessary to brush lightly over the surface so as to knock off any top dressing which remains on the foliage.

The benefits of top dressing

Grass growth is denser — the formation of new shoots is stimulated and the layer of top dressing promotes the development of runners

Minor hollows are removed so that a truer surface is obtained

The soil surface is gradually built up — thatch tends to decompose in this layer and drought resistance is improved

The water-holding capacity of sandy soil is improved

Drainage in heavy soil is improved, especially if spiking is carried out as a pre-treatment

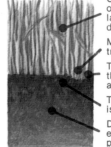

LAWN CARE   FEEDING

During late spring and summer, the rapid growth of grass means that frequent mowing is essential. The dangers of allowing the grass to grow too tall have already been pointed out, so the turf must be kept at the recommended height (see page 31) no matter how actively it is growing.

On this basis it might seem that feeding the lawn is a foolish thing to do. Isn't it hard enough to keep the grass down without forcing it to grow more quickly? Is it *really* worth the extra cost of fertilizer and the need for extra cutting just to make the grass look greener?

The simple answer is that the plant foods contained in a compound lawn fertilizer do much more than make the grass look greener. Their main task is to produce closely-knit turf in which neither weeds nor moss can obtain a ready foothold. The grass is indeed made more attractive because of its deeper green colour, but equally important is the build up of resistance to drought and disease.

Mowing is a serious drain on the soil's reserve of major plant foods. Nitrogen becomes exhausted quite quickly — phosphates and potash more slowly. Unless the reserves are replaced the grass turns pale and the turf becomes thin and sparse. Fertilizer is needed — not too little but not too much. Good lawn management calls for a regular lawn feeding programme.

WHAT THE LAWN NEEDS

NUTRIENT	USE ON THE LAWN	EFFECT	TYPICAL SOURCES	BEST TIME TO APPLY
NITROGEN Greens grass Stimulates leaf growth	**ESSENTIAL** This plant food runs out before the others — at least one application is essential every season	The production of rich green and vigorous turf is stimulated. All spring and summer feeds should have more nitrogen than any other element — if not, don't buy it. The nitrogen may be quick- or slow-acting — the package should tell you which. Active growth is *not* wanted during winter — nitrogen content of an autumn lawn feed should be low.	Spring or summer compound lawn fertilizer Lawn Sand Sulphate of ammonia Dried blood	**Spring and Summer**
PHOSPHATES Build up the root system	**ESSENTIAL** Some phosphates should be applied once every season	The production of a vigorous root system is stimulated. The result is that growth starts earlier in the spring, fresh reserves of food and water can be tapped in the summer, and side-shooting is promoted in early autumn.	Autumn compound lawn fertilizer Bone Meal Super-phosphates	**Spring or Autumn**
POTASH Stimulates healthy growth	**DESIRABLE** It is useful to apply potash once every season	Not as vital as nitrogen or phosphates but there is evidence that its use 'hardens' the grass and so makes it less susceptible to drought, disease and discoloration.	Spring or autumn compound lawn fertilizer Sulphate of potash	**Spring or Autumn**

FERTILIZERS AND THE WEATHER

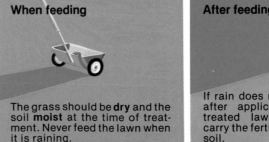

Before feeding

Check the weather forecast. If possible, pick a time when showery weather is likely. Avoid feeding during prolonged dry weather. If treatment must be done at such times, water thoroughly shortly before application and then treat as soon as the foliage is dry.

When feeding

The grass should be **dry** and the soil **moist** at the time of treatment. Never feed the lawn when it is raining.

After feeding

If rain does not fall for 2 days after application, water the treated lawn thoroughly to carry the fertilizer down into the soil.

WHAT FERTILIZERS TO USE

The gardener can be excused for being confused. There seem to be as many feeding programmes as there are books on lawn care and a wide array of products are advertised in the gardening magazines. But this does not mean that the feeding of grass is a haphazard affair without any rules — all good schemes have the same basic foundation. It is only the details which differ.

Nitrogen enters the feeding story in spring, once the grass has started to grow strongly. It is usual to give the first dressing in the form of a compound fertilizer containing both phosphates and potash in addition to the nitrogen. Some proprietary brands contain both quick- and slow-acting forms of nitrogen — use a combined fertilizer-weedkiller if weeds are widespread on the lawn.

If the lawn appears pale and is not growing vigorously in June or July then summer feeding is necessary. There is no general agreement on the form that it should take — some experts recommend ½ oz of sulphate of ammonia per sq. yard but this can result in scorch in hot and dry weather. Others prefer a urea-based liquid fertilizer which provides a quick green-up without the risk of scorch. Some gardeners believe that a second treatment with a nitrogen-rich compound fertilizer is the best thing to use at this stage.

Quick-acting nitrogen should not be used once autumn arrives. An autumn fertilizer containing phosphates, potash and some slow-acting nitrogen is useful but not essential. Consider autumn feeding if the lawn has been badly affected by summer drought.

SPRING	SUMMER	AUTUMN
Essential	Desirable	Occasionally desirable

HOW TO USE THEM

Whichever method of application is used, even distribution is essential or patchiness and perhaps scorch will be the result. You should try to devise a way of marking to avoid overlapping or missed areas unless you use a product which shows up on the turf.

HAND APPLICATION	Hand application is still the most widely used method. Apply half up and down the lawn, and then go back over the area crosswise with the remaining half. Patchy application is always a danger — evenness is improved if the fertilizer is bulked up with sand, but do not do this if the feed is blended with weedkiller.
HAND-HELD DISTRIBUTOR	There are two basic types. The first is a spreader nozzle which is screwed on to the pack and allows the product to sprinkle out as the container is carried along. The second is an applicator on which a handle is cranked to distribute the fertilizer held in the hopper.
LIQUID DILUTOR	Soluble fertilizers are available. The quick-acting solution can be applied through a watering can, but this is a slow job even on an average-sized lawn. A much better method of application is to use a hose-end dilutor which will treat large areas very quickly and effectively.
WHEELED DISTRIBUTOR	This wheeled machine speeds up fertilizer application, and is capable of producing more even results than hand application. However, if used carelessly a 'tramline' effect is produced due to missed or double-dosed strips of turf. After use clean out the distributor thoroughly — damp fertilizer can be corrosive.

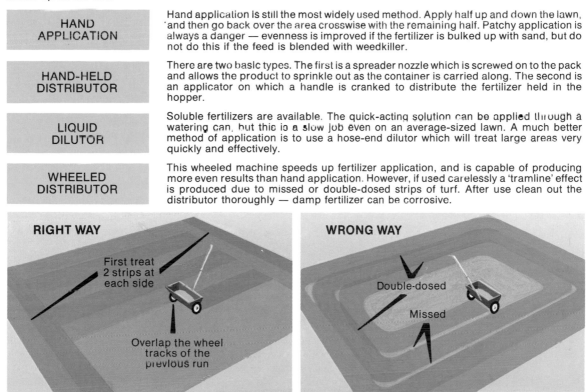

RIGHT WAY
First treat 2 strips at each side
Overlap the wheel tracks of the previous run

WRONG WAY
Double-dosed
Missed

LAWN CARE | WATERING

THE PROBLEM

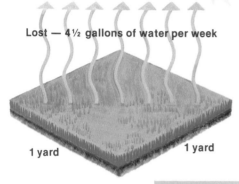

Lost — 4½ gallons of water per week

1 yard   1 yard

Grass cannot live without water. The amount of rainfall in this country is usually sufficient to keep the roots well supplied with moisture. But prolonged dry spells do occasionally occur in late spring and summer, and the need for extra water arises.

On the established lawn, the first tell-tale signs of drought appear as soon as the top four inches have dried out. If water, in the form of rain or irrigation, is not forthcoming then the grass turns straw-coloured and unsightly. In extreme cases the grasses may die — which can occur quite quickly with drought-susceptible varieties such as annual meadow grass.

Lawn grasses are rarely killed by drought in Britain, and recovery takes place once the rains return. But there is a hidden handicap — some weeds, such as clover and yarrow, are much more drought-resistant than grass and so they are able to spread amid the weakened grass.

TACKLING THE PROBLEM

1 Increase drought resistance

You should use all the available techniques which create a deep and vigorous root system. This will increase drought resistance, and there will be times when you will have to rely solely on the turf's natural ability to survive in dry conditions ... Water Authorities have the maddening habit of banning hosepipes and sprinklers just when the lawn's need becomes desperate!

- Spike the turf in autumn where compaction is a problem (page 45)
- Top dress in autumn, especially after spiking (page 35)
- Never cut below the recommended height (page 31). Let the grass grow a little longer in dry weather
- Leave the clippings on the lawn in times of drought
- Feed regularly. Use a phosphate-containing fertilizer at least once a year to promote root activity
- Remove thatch by scarifying in autumn (page 43)

2 Water the lawn thoroughly

The purpose of irrigation is to refill the soil's reservoir of water once it has begun to run dry. Unfortunately it is not just a matter of turning on the hosepipe and flooding the turf until it is waterlogged. Too much as well as too little has its dangers, and so does watering too frequently. Follow the rules below and on the next page to keep your lawn green and healthy when the dry weather arrives.

WHEN TO WATER

The first sign of trouble is the loss of 'springiness' in the grass — this is the best time to start. The next stage in the effect of drought is a change of colour — the bright green fades and a grey-green hue appears. Don't wait any longer before you start watering. Delay will mean that the grass will turn yellow and then brown, and both moss and weeds will flourish when the water balance is once again restored.

Before you turn on the water for the first time, examine the surface. If it is baked hard or is covered with a strawy mat of dead vegetation it is a good idea to prick the turf to aid penetration (see page 45).

Obviously the best time to water is when the weather is cool so that evaporation will be at a minimum. Evening or early morning is the best time.

HOW OFTEN TO WATER

This will depend upon the soil type and the weather. Lawns on sandy soil are more affected by drought than those on heavy soil, and so more frequent watering is necessary in light-land areas. Obviously more frequent watering will be necessary during a heat wave than in a cool dry spell.

There are no exact rules governing the frequency of watering. As a simple guide, water once a week under ordinary dry conditions. In abnormally hot weather or on free-draining soil this can be increased to twice a week, and in cool weather it can be decreased to every 10 days.

The guiding principle is to allow the lawn to dry out to some extent between waterings so as to let air in and stimulate deep root development. Sprinkling every day or two is bad practice — it will lead to the spread of moss and pearlwort and the production of a shallow rooting system.

HOW TO WATER

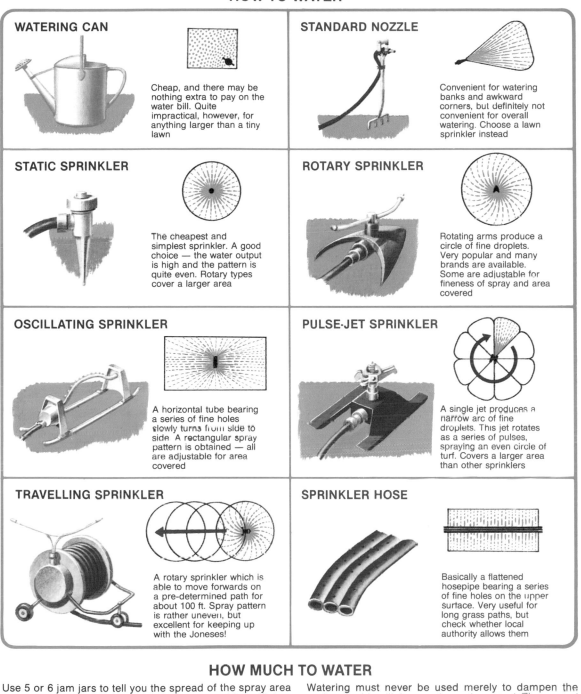

WATERING CAN

Cheap, and there may be nothing extra to pay on the water bill. Quite impractical, however, for anything larger than a tiny lawn

STANDARD NOZZLE

Convenient for watering banks and awkward corners, but definitely not convenient for overall watering. Choose a lawn sprinkler instead

STATIC SPRINKLER

The cheapest and simplest sprinkler. A good choice — the water output is high and the pattern is quite even. Rotary types cover a larger area

ROTARY SPRINKLER

Rotating arms produce a circle of fine droplets. Very popular and many brands are available. Some are adjustable for fineness of spray and area covered

OSCILLATING SPRINKLER

A horizontal tube bearing a series of fine holes slowly turns from side to side. A rectangular spray pattern is obtained — all are adjustable for area covered

PULSE-JET SPRINKLER

A single jet produces a narrow arc of fine droplets. This jet rotates as a series of pulses, spraying an even circle of turf. Covers a larger area than other sprinklers

TRAVELLING SPRINKLER

A rotary sprinkler which is able to move forwards on a pre-determined path for about 100 ft. Spray pattern is rather uneven, but excellent for keeping up with the Joneses!

SPRINKLER HOSE

Basically a flattened hosepipe bearing a series of fine holes on the upper surface. Very useful for long grass paths, but check whether local authority allows them

HOW MUCH TO WATER

Use 5 or 6 jam jars to tell you the spread of the spray area and the number of minutes required to provide sufficient water over the irrigated zone.

Watering must never be used merely to dampen the surface — this will do more harm than good. The ground should be soaked to a depth of at least 4 in.

 ½ inch of water = 2¼ gallons of water, the minimum which should be applied

 1 inch of water = 4½ gallons of water, the amount needed to replace the water lost during a week of dry weather

LAWN CARE TRIMMING

After using a sharp and well-set mower, the lawn will appear neat and tidy . . . but there is still another job to do. Trimming calls for removing all the overgrown bits of grass which the mower couldn't reach. Once this was a matter of using long-handled shears, but nowadays there is a wide array of hand- and motor-driven trimmers. As described on these two pages, some are a real boon in the large lawn whereas others are no quicker or easier to use than a pair of shears. All should be handled with care.

In the traditional square or rectangular lawn with a flower bed or two and surrounded by paths and borders, there may be little or no horizontal trimming to do. But vertical trimming will certainly be necessary to maintain a neat edge. Where the edges crumble easily, it is a good idea to insert an edging strip. This is a strip of wood, concrete, aluminium or plastic set below grass level to preserve the lawn edge and to stop creeping grasses from spreading into the lawn.

HORIZONTAL TRIMMING

There may be many places in your lawn where the mower cannot reach — around the base of trees, under spreading shrubs and along fences and walls. You will need a horizontal trimmer, and the choice is listed below. Remember that the need to trim can often be eliminated by leaving a space between the grass and the obstacle so that the mower can go over the edge of the turf.

LONG-HANDLED LAWN SHEARS

Until recently these shears were the basic method of cutting long grass growing in awkward places. There are obvious advantages — you work in an upright position, there is nothing to go wrong and they are cheaper than powered trimmers. When they are sharp and properly cared for they are relatively quick to use.

NYLON CORD TRIMMER

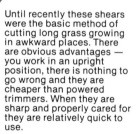

The most recently introduced of the horizontal trimmers, but it has quickly gained in popularity and is now the best-selling type. The nylon cord trimmer (or 'strimmer') is nearly always driven by electricity and is quick and easy to use — the replaceable nylon cord whirling at high speed to cut through the grass. Excellent for steep banks and other awkward areas but there are minor drawbacks — the cord rapidly wears when it hits solid objects or has to cut through long tough grass, and you should wear goggles.

SHORT-HANDLED LAWN SHEARS

It may seem at first sight that there is no point in buying a pair of shears which require you to bend down to cut unmown grass. Most people obviously prefer to stand upright for the trimming operation, but there are others who do prefer to get close and see what they are doing. These lightweight shears with their spring-loaded short blades are operated with one hand. They are slower to use than the long-handled type, but are definitely worth considering if you only have the grass growing around a tree or a similar tiny area to worry about.

CORDLESS TRIMMER

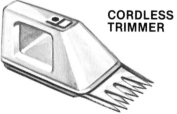

An overgrown pair of hair clippers which can be hand-held or fitted with an extension handle. Motor-driven but without a cable to worry about, the cut is excellent and they work at about the same speed as a good pair of long-handled lawn shears. An attractive proposition when described this way in the catalogues, but you must remember that they are battery-driven and the cut with one charge is only 10 – 20 sq. yards.

VERTICAL TRIMMING

Vertical trimming, or edging, is necessary at regular intervals to maintain a neat appearance. Clippings should be removed from beds or borders after edging to prevent the bits of grass from rooting in the soil. There is a choice between long-handled shears and mechanical edgers — ordinary hand shears are only suitable for very small lawns. Remember that the need for vertical trimming can be reduced or even eliminated by installing a mowing strip — see page 9 for details.

After the first spring mowing

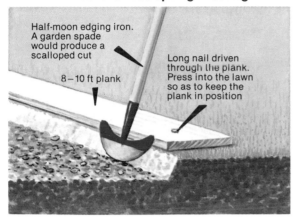

Half-moon edging iron. A garden spade would produce a scalloped cut

8–10 ft plank

Long nail driven through the plank. Press into the lawn so as to keep the plank in position

After subsequent mowings

Use shears or a mechanical edger — do not use a half moon edging iron

Maintain the slight slope created by the half-moon edging iron

LONG-HANDLED EDGING SHEARS

The age-old way of maintaining a trim edge, and still considered to be the best method unless you have a very large lawn. If the shears are well-set and sharp, they should be quick and easy to use, but you must make sure that their length is right for you. Always feel their weight and test the cutting action before you buy — the handle length may be as short as 32 in. or as long as 44 in.

Some models have a grass-catching attachment — a time-saver in some cases but a positive nuisance in others where the mowing edge is shallow and narrow. At the end of the season make sure you oil the nuts and bolts as well as the blades before putting the shears away for their winter rest.

ROLLER EDGER

A disc of sharpened spikes rotates against a fixed blade as you push the trimmer along the edge of the lawn. In general a roller edger is no quicker to use nor does it give as good a cut as a pair of long-handled shears. Some people find this piece of equipment difficult to use — try it before deciding to buy one. In general, your choice should be between a pair of edging shears and a power-driven edger.

POWER-DRIVEN EDGER

If you have a large lawn with firm edges and you find the use of edging shears particularly tiring then you can consider a battery-driven or electric-driven edger. It will not make the job quicker but you are spared a lot of physical effort. You will need some practice before you learn the art of keeping this machine moving in a straight line along the edge and of course they are not cheap — a power-driven edger will cost you more than a small electric mower.

LAWN CARE | RAKING AND BRUSHING

Lawns gather a great deal of rubbish during the year — fallen leaves, twigs, dead grass, worm casts and so on. No single tool is ideal for the removal of all types of debris — the right piece of equipment depends on the job that has to be done. Leaves in autumn are effectively dealt with by the gentle action of bristles or rubber teeth — a group of tools known as sweepers. In recent years the vacuum/blower has appeared as an alternative to the sweeper.

At the other end of the scale are the tools which dig firmly into the turf and drag out the layer of dead matted grass known as thatch — these tools are the scarifiers. Between these two types of lawn tool are the wire rakes, which form an essential part of the lawn owner's armoury of equipment. The electrically driven Lawnraker is a useful piece of equipment. It has three settings — low for scarifying, medium for raking and high for sweeping up leaves. The debris is thrown into a front-mounted grass box.

BRUSHING

The use of a broom or broom-like tool to clean the surface of the turf

USED IN SPRING to remove dew and raindrops from grass foliage and to spread worm casts before mowing. The initial clean-up before the first spring mowing should be done by gentle raking and not by brushing.	**AN OCCASIONAL TREATMENT; USEFUL WHEN THE LAWN FOLIAGE IS WET**
USED IN LATE SPRING AND SUMMER to remove dew and raindrops from grass foliage and to spread worm casts before mowing. It is also used to lift the grass leaves and weed stems for efficient cutting. This treatment is more gentle than raking — a definite advantage when treating turf before the end of June.	**AN OCCASIONAL TREATMENT; USEFUL WHEN THE LAWN FOLIAGE IS WET**
USED IN AUTUMN AND WINTER to remove leaves and other debris from the lawn. It may have to be carried out several times to ensure that a grass-smothering blanket of fallen leaves does not remain on the lawn over winter.	**AN ALTERNATIVE TREATMENT TO SCARIFYING OR RAKING IN SEPTEMBER** **AN ALTERNATIVE TREATMENT TO RAKING IN LATE AUTUMN**

VACUUMING

The use of a vacuum/blower to clean the surface of the turf

A range of vacuum/blowers has appeared — these hand-held or wheeled machines can be set to blow leaves and other debris into heaps or to vacuum up leaves, small twigs etc. into a collecting bag. They are useful for large lawns with a serious autumn leaf problem but are not really necessary for the average-sized lawn.

VACUUM/BLOWER

BESOM

LAWN BRUSH

MECHANICAL SWEEPER

RAKING

The use of a spring-tine rake or a split-cane rake with very little downward pressure

USED IN SPRING to remove winter debris, to break up small amounts of thatch and to lift the grass leaves and weed stems for efficient cutting.	**AN ESSENTIAL TREATMENT**
USED IN LATE SPRING AND SUMMER to collect up grass clippings after mowing. It is also used to lift up the leaves and stems of patches of troublesome weed. Never rake the lawn vigorously at this stage — consider brushing as a gentler alternative.	**AN OCCASIONAL TREATMENT WHICH IS BY NO MEANS ESSENTIAL IF THE LAWN IS FREE FROM DEBRIS**
USED IN AUTUMN to remove leaves and other debris and to break up small amounts of thatch. If thatch is serious then you will have to scarify instead. After raking as part of an autumn maintenance programme it may still be necessary to brush the lawn in winter to remove fallen leaves.	**AN ALTERNATIVE TREATMENT TO SCARIFYING OR BRUSHING**

SPRING-TINE
RAKE

The Thatch Problem

The make-up of this fibrous layer which forms on the surface of many lawns is described briefly on page 6. When this layer is an inch or more in thickness a semi-waterproof cover is created. In summer it impedes proper aeration, and the downward passage of rain is restricted.

The effect in autumn is even more serious. The thickening of the turf which should normally take place in September is inhibited, and the constantly wet organic blanket encourages disease.

Thatch is a problem of the established lawn. In most cases occasional raking and brushing will prevent its build up, but in very acid or poorly drained soils the extra protection afforded by an annual top dressing (see page 35) may be necessary in the fight against thatch.

Where a thick layer of thatch is already present, aeration (see page 44) will break through the layer, but scarifying is essential for its removal. If the affected area is large, you can hire a powered scarifier from your local machinery dealer.

SCARIFYING

The use of a rake or rake-like tool with considerable downward pressure

DO NOT USE IN SPRING. Heavy raking which tears into the grass will damage the lawn. The grass does not produce side-shoots at this stage and so scarifying will open up the turf and make it vulnerable to weed invasion.	**NOT RECOMMENDED!**
USED IN LATE SPRING AND SUMMER to remove patches of dead moss which have been killed by Lawn Sand or a proprietary moss killer. Never scarify the whole of the lawn at this stage.	**A MOSS-REMOVAL TREATMENT**
USED IN EARLY AUTUMN to remove debris from the lawn and to remove thick thatch. Early September is the best time for scarifying, and the removal of thatch at this stage will stimulate the production of the side-shoots and runners which the grass plants develop at this time of the year. If moss is present, use a moss killer a week or two before scarifying. Where a large amount of thatch has been removed it will be necessary to apply grass seed to the bare areas.	**AN ESSENTIAL TREATMENT IF THICK THATCH IS PRESENT**

SPRING-TINE
RAKE

GARDEN
RAKE

SCRAKE

LAWN CARE | AERATING

The basic idea behind aerating is perfectly simple. Holes or slits are created so that air and water can penetrate beneath the surface. This definition is perhaps the only simple thing about aeration. It is a difficult job to do properly over a large area, it is not easy to decide whether it is necessary in some lawns and it is not simple to choose the right equipment. So read this section carefully and you may be able to save yourself the hours of backache recommended by some books.

The basic purpose of driving air channels deep into the turf is to break through the compaction layer which occurs at about two or three inches beneath the surface. It is not always there — it builds up when the soil particles are squeezed together by heavy traffic — children's feet around a play area, the central strip of a pathway, and so on. This compaction layer in heavy soil will seriously damage the grass, and so you must break into it by means of **spiking**.

Spiking consists of driving solid or hollow spikes (technically known as *tines*) into the surface to a depth of at least three inches. A vital air exchange takes place — oxygen, so vital for root growth, gets into the compacted layer and carbon dioxide, so harmful as it inhibits the passage of water into the roots, escapes. There is more to it than just air exchange — water can now get down to the roots and this is important in both summer and winter. In times of drought the roots will die if starved of water — in winter the surface will become affected by moss and thatch if rain cannot percolate into the soil.

From the above description you may be tempted to rush out and spike every inch of your lawn. Don't. It is a back-breaking job to treat large areas and if not necessary it can do more harm than good. The rule is to spike only when compaction is obvious, to do the work in early autumn and to carry it out once a year if you use a garden fork and no more than once every three years if you use a hollow-tine fork.

In addition to the compaction layer, most lawns possess a mat layer. This is an accumulation of dead matter and compacted soil in the surface inch of the turf. **Pricking** breaks through this layer, and this is a useful technique in spring and summer. You must remember, however, that pricking will not relieve deep-seated compaction.

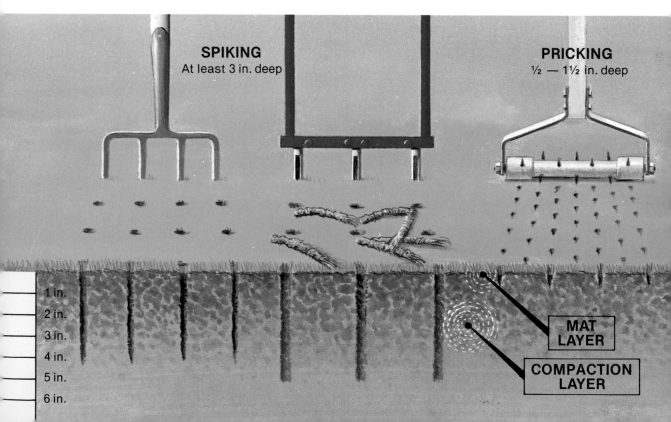

SPIKING
At least 3 in. deep

PRICKING
½ — 1½ in. deep

MAT LAYER

COMPACTION LAYER

1 in.
2 in.
3 in.
4 in.
5 in.
6 in.

SPIKING

GARDEN FORK

HOLLOW-TINE FORK

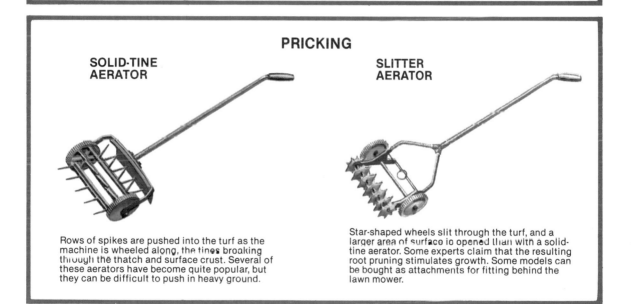

Ideal for small areas, especially if the soil is sandy or loamy. Drive the fork in vertically to a depth of about 4 in., rock it back and forth *gently* and then pull it out vertically. Work away from the treated area, leaving about 6 in. between the lines of holes.

Ideal for heavy soils—never use on sandy soils. Each hollow tine takes out a core of earth, so wide air channels are created and the compaction of the sides of the holes is avoided. Sweep up and remove the cores. Do not use this technique more than once every 3 years.

MECHANICAL SPIKER

Many types of motorised spikers are available, bearing solid tines, chisel-shaped tines, hollow tines or deep slitter tines. If you have a large area to treat it is well worth hiring a large motor-driven aerator for the day.

PRICKING

SOLID-TINE AERATOR

SLITTER AERATOR

Rows of spikes are pushed into the turf as the machine is wheeled along, the tines breaking through the thatch and surface crust. Several of these aerators have become quite popular, but they can be difficult to push in heavy ground.

Star-shaped wheels slit through the turf, and a larger area of surface is opened than with a solid-tine aerator. Some experts claim that the resulting root pruning stimulates growth. Some models can be bought as attachments for fitting behind the lawn mower.

WHERE TO AERATE

Spiking
Spike only those areas which are showing symptoms of compaction. Look for two or more of the following symptoms:
● Waterlogging after rain
● Unusually rapid browning in dry weather
● Moss of the trailing type (see page 78)
● Bare patches due to heavy traffic
● Poor grass vigour

Pricking
Prick the whole area of the lawn in summer if water applied in dry weather does not rapidly soak into the surface.

WHEN TO AERATE

Spiking
September is the best month. Choose a day when the soil is moist. Scarify first, then top dress afterwards. This treatment will improve drainage, and the new roots formed will render the lawn more resistant to drought in the following summer.

Pricking
Spring or summer, before feeding or irrigating. Choose a day when the soil is moist.

LAWN CARE LIMING

Lime shortage is very rarely a problem in the lawn. The only time you should consider liming is when there are unmistakable signs of lime deficiency. The grass will be thin and sparse, and the turf will be overrun by woodrush, sheep's sorrel and moss. An acidity test should be carried out — the pH will be below 5.5. If all of these signs are present, apply 2 oz of ground limestone per sq. yard in autumn or winter — do not use ordinary garden lime.

If the signs are not present, *don't lime*. The use of chalk, limestone or garden lime on an ordinary lawn will quickly lead to deterioration. Weeds, worms and fungal diseases increase and fine grasses decline.

As a general rule it is the gardener's job to increase and not decrease acidity. This is done by using Lawn Sand and by incorporating peat in the autumn top dressing.

LAWN CARE ROLLING

In the hands of the skilled greenkeeper a roller does useful work by consolidating the surface of sports turf and by producing an attractive 'face'. In the hands of the ordinary gardener a roller will almost certainly do more harm than good.

The purpose of a roller is to firm the surface of an already smooth lawn. It is totally wrong to use it to iron out the bumps — it usually makes matters worse by depressing the hollows even further.

Only in the spring does the roller have a role to play in established turf. The purpose of this early spring rolling is to reconsolidate the turf which has been lifted by frost. If you have a mower fitted with a back roller, all you have to do is to go over the lawn with the cutter head held high by pressing down on the handle.

If you have a mower without a back roller then you may have to consider borrowing or hiring a light roller if frost has lifted the turf. Make sure it doesn't weigh more than two cwt. and choose a day when the grass is dry and the soil is moist. Brush off worm casts, surface debris, etc., before rolling.

LAWN CARE READING

A distinctly odd-sounding method of lawn care, which you will not find in the text books. However, reading gardening magazines *is* part of lawn care these days because the equipment scene is constantly changing. Each year new mowers, new trimmers, new grass varieties, new chemicals and new types of turf appear — reading articles and advertisements is the standard method of keeping up-to-date.

CHAPTER 4

LAWN TROUBLES

UNDER-TREE TROUBLE
Moss, bare patches and sparse grass.
See page 8

ALGAE
Black slime on waterlogged turf.
See page 51

MOLE HILLS
Large mounds of earth. Long raised ridges may be present.
See page 49

SMALL HILLS
Small mounds of earth. Ants or mining bees.
See page 49

EARTHWORM CASTS
Small mounds of earth. Soil sticky.
See page 48

BROWN PATCHES
See pages 80–81

LICHEN
Brown or grey overlapping plates, white underneath.
See page 51

WATERLOGGING
Try spiking (see page 44) followed by top dressing. If the trouble is not cured, create a soakaway at the lowest part of the lawn — see page 94

BIRDS
Starlings actively pecking the turf usually indicate leatherjacket attack.
See page 48

DAISIES
See page 71

BARE PATCHES
See page 83

MOSS
See page 78

TOADSTOOLS & FAIRY RINGS
Circles of dark green grass may be present.
See page 51

BUMPS & HOLLOWS
See page 82

WEEDS
See pages 52–77

PALE GREEN GRASS
Usual cause is nitrogen starvation — apply Lawn Tonic or sulphate of ammonia.
See page 36

PEARLWORT
Moss-like weed with tiny white flowers.
See page 71

WEED GRASSES
See page 79

THIN & SPARSE GRASS
Various causes — incorrect mowing (page 31), starvation (page 36), poor aeration (page 44) and deep shade (no cure).

RIBBING
See page 86

BROKEN EDGES
See page 82

CLOVER
See page 64

Pets

In some parts of the world the lawn owner has to wage a constant battle against a variety of underground pests. Fortunately this threat to the roots and stem bases is much less serious in Britain, but we still do have our share of disfiguring insect and animal pests. The most widespread is the earthworm, which unfortunately can no longer be controlled by chemical means. The pet bitch is also a difficult problem, as her eradication is quite unthinkable!

EARTHWORMS

Earthworms do not directly attack turf — in fact they are supposed to have a beneficial effect by producing drainage holes within the soil. Many types of earthworms do play a valuable role in the flower and vegetable garden, but the cast-forming species in the lawn are not efficient soil aerators. The harm caused by the mounds of coiled sticky earth which they produce far outweighs any benefits.

These worm casts are, of course, an eyesore but the hidden dangers are much more serious. When the casts are flattened by feet or mower, the lawn surface is rendered uneven and the fine grasses below them are stifled. The muddy, slippery surface is then open to weed invasion. In addition a large population of earthworms encourages moles to come to your garden.

Avoiding and curing the problem

If your soil is rather heavy and rich in organic matter, then the surface can be quite quickly ruined by earthworm activity. Always remove the clippings when mowing, and try to increase the acidity of the turf. This calls for dressing it with peat each year, using a fertilizer (such as Lawn Sand) which contains sulphate of ammonia and, of course, never applying a dressing of lime.

Casts are most likely to appear in spring or autumn in mild damp weather. If they are numerous, scatter them when they are dry with a besom before attempting to mow. Until quite recently chemical preparations were available for the control of earthworms. Mowrah meal was the traditional remedy and this was followed by carbaryl, but these pesticides are no longer sold. This means that you will have to rely on non-chemical and indirect methods to stop casts spoiling your lawn. The two techniques are brushing the dry casts away plus the use of acidifying treatments such as Lawn Sand.

LEATHERJACKETS

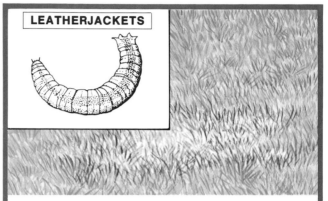

Leatherjackets are the worst of all insect pests — in poorly drained lawns after a wet autumn the damage can be extremely serious. Crane flies (daddy-long-legs) lay their eggs in late summer in the turf — the grubs hatch out in autumn and they cause the damage. During spring they feed on the roots and stem bases, resulting in patches of yellow or brown grass which are most noticeable during dry weather in early summer.

Starlings actively pecking in the turf are a sign of leatherjacket attack. Check by watering a patch of the lawn and then covering it overnight with black polythene sheeting. In the morning look for the tell-tale 1 in. long grey or brown legless grubs.

Avoiding and curing the problem

Aerating the lawn to improve drainage (see page 44) will help to prevent attacks, but more action is needed in areas where leatherjackets are a regular pest. Water in an insecticide containing HCH in autumn, or use a product based on leatherjacket-killing nematodes in spring.

CHAFER GRUBS

The flat curved grubs of garden chafers gnaw at the roots during spring and summer, but they are a much less common problem than leatherjackets. Small brown patches of dying grass appear, which can be pulled away quite easily.

Avoiding and curing the problem

Special preventative measures are rarely needed, except in sandy areas. Rolling in spring will crush the grubs, and a nematode-based insecticide used for leatherjacket control will also keep this pest in check.

MOLES

One of the saddest sights in gardening is to see a fine even lawn suddenly ruined by moles. Large heaps of earth appear overnight, and the underground activity leads to long raised ridges or sunken lines of collapsed tunnels.

Attacks by these small black animals are most likely in sandy stone-free soils and in lawns which receive little attention or traffic. Few lawns, however, can be considered immune.

Avoiding and curing the problem
Prevention is most certainly better than cure when dealing with moles. Their main diet consists of earthworms, and so reducing the population (see page 48) is advisable if you have seen signs of mole activity in your neighbourhood.

Getting rid of moles once they have invaded your lawn is not easy. All sorts of techniques are described in text books and magazines, and all have had their successes — moth balls, burning paper, creosote, disinfectant and proprietary smoke cartridges inserted in the main runs. If one deterrent fails try another type, but the moles tend to return if they are not killed.

Trapping is an effective method of eradication, but it is a skilful task. The secret is to place the correct trap (half barrel or caliper type) along a permanent run (not under an old mole hill) with as little disturbance as possible. If you can, use the services of a professional mole catcher. Poisoning is an alternative method of killing moles — this job *must* be left to the professional.

BITCHES

Dogs are no respecters of lawns, and bitch urine has a scorching effect on turf. The brown patches are roughly circular in outline, with a ring of dark lush grass surrounding each patch. The effect is worst in dry weather.

Avoiding and curing the problem
The problem is both annoying and frustrating, because so little can be done to prevent or cure it. There are no effective repellents which can be used to treat a whole lawn, and the only thing you can do is to water the patch copiously. If the brown area remains an eyesore, re-seeding or re-turfing is the only answer.

ANTS

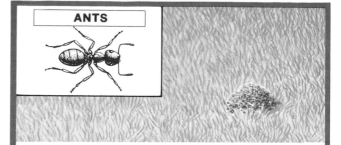

Unlike worm casts, ant hills are characteristic of sandy soils and they appear during the heat of the summer. They are not as harmful to the turf as the casts of earthworms, but they do disfigure the surface and they can make mowing difficult. The yellow turf ant is the usual culprit, and its activity below the surface can cause some root damage and leaf yellowing.

Avoiding and curing the problem
Scatter the hills with a besom before mowing. If they are numerous, locate the nest and open it up with a spade — liberally sprinkle an anti-ant dust over the exposed surface.

MINING BEES

The mining bee is stingless, and makes its nest under lawns and paths. The excavated soil is deposited as a small conical mound on the surface — at first glance it looks like an ant hill, but there is a characteristic crater at the top.

Avoiding and curing the problem
The small mounds produced by mining bees rarely require any drastic action — merely scatter the earth before mowing. In a few areas, however, they do appear in large numbers in the same spot year after year — in this case dust the mounds with HCH in April.

BIRDS

Birds are not a serious problem on the established lawn, although starlings will occasionally tear out tufts of grass in their search for grubs, and rooks may cause minor damage in their search for nesting material. Sparrows, however, can be a problem on newly-seeded lawns, as they use the seed bed as a dust bath.

Avoiding and curing the problem
The basic answer to the bird problem is to get rid of the underground grubs which attract them — see the sections on *leatherjackets* and *chafer grubs*. Always treat seed with a bird repellent before sowing and criss-cross re-seeded patches with black thread.

Diseases

Lawns, like all living things, can suffer from disease. Most of these diseases are caused by fungi and some, such as fusarium patch, can be killers. The division between weeds and diseases should be a clear-cut one, but it isn't ... some experts treat lichens and algae as weeds, because they are indeed primitive forms of plant life, but in this book they are treated as diseases. The term *weed* is restricted to the unwanted green-leaved plants which all too often invade our lawns.

FUSARIUM PATCH (SNOW MOULD)

Fusarium patch is the commonest fungal disease of British lawns — it is most prevalent in autumn and also in spring after long-lying snow has melted. The first sign of trouble is a small area of yellowing grass — the patch increases in size to about 1 ft across, and these patches may merge to form extensive brown areas in which the grass is killed. In moist weather the edges of the diseased areas may be covered with white or pale pink fluffy mould.

Avoiding and curing the problem
Curing this disease is never easy, so do all you can to avoid infection. Do not use a nitrogen-rich fertilizer in autumn or winter, spike the turf regularly and never walk on the lawn when it is covered with snow. The treatment is a systemic fungicide such as carbendazim. Mix with water and apply at the first sign of disease.

RED THREAD (CORTICIUM DISEASE)

Fine-leaved grasses which are rarely if ever fed are susceptible to attack. In late summer or autumn look for irregular patches of bleached grass which later take on a pinkish tinge. Look more closely in moist weather and you will find small red needle-like growths standing up from the leaves of grass. Red thread does not kill the turf but it is unsightly until the bleached patches recover.

Avoiding and curing the problem
Good lawn care is the secret. Feed your lawn in spring or summer every year, spike the turf and avoid mowing too closely if your soil is sandy. The treatment is a systemic fungicide such as carbendazim. Mix with water and apply at the first sign of disease.

OPHIOBOLUS PATCH

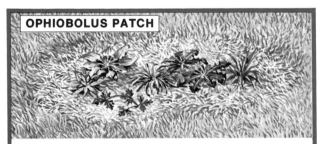

This killer disease is fortunately not common. It affects the Bent grasses (see page 12) and is usually associated with poor drainage, underfeeding and overliming. Ophiobolus begins as a small sunken area which steadily increases in size, year by year, until it reaches several feet across with a bleached ring of grass at the outer edge. The characteristic feature is the colonisation of the central dead area by weeds and coarse grasses.

Avoiding and curing the problem
Apply Lawn Sand in the spring, never lime unless necessary and spike the lawn in autumn. As soon as the disease has been positively identified, the patch should be re-turfed whilst it is still small.

DOLLAR SPOT

If your lawn is made up of utility-grade grasses, then dollar spot will not trouble you. It is a disease of fine-leaved turf, and is usually only serious in Cumberland turf. The patches are circular, about 1–2 in. across, and straw-coloured or golden brown. A luxury lawn can be badly disfigured — the patches coalesce and large areas may be affected.

Avoiding and curing the problem
If your lawn is rich in Creeping Red Fescue, take special care to avoid dollar spot attack. Feed with a nitrogen-rich fertilizer each spring. Spike the turf during the autumn months and remove the thatch which builds up around the stem bases. The only treatment is a systemic fungicide such as carbendazim. Mix the powder with water and apply to the affected area at the first sign of disease.

TOADSTOOLS and FAIRY RINGS

Many types of toadstools are capable of growing in turf, and a few scattered here and there over the lawn are not particularly objectionable. The usual cause is buried organic debris, and removing this will often eliminate a small clump of toadstools.

With a few types of toadstools a ring is formed, and this grows wider and wider each year. If the grass is not discoloured by the underground fungal growth, you have a Grade 3 fairy ring and remedial action is not necessary. Some toadstools, such as puffballs and mushrooms, produce a Grade 2 fairy ring which is recognized by the dark green grass at the edge of the ring. The effect can be unsightly but control is very difficult, so the best course of action is to keep the lawn well fed. In this way the colour of the ring is masked by the overall rich green of the lawn.

The toadstool *Marasmius oreades* produces a Grade 1 fairy ring, and this truly is a problem. Two dark green rings are formed, as in the illustration, and the space between them is bare and moss-ridden. The ring may be small or it may cover the whole lawn, and control is always difficult.

Remove all pieces of wood from the soil before making a lawn and keep it vigorous by following the rules of proper care laid down in Chapter 3. Despite doing all the right things, a Grade 1 fairy ring may still appear. Claims for a miracle cure occasionally appear but no water-on technique has proved reliable, as the underground fungal growth waterproofs the soil. You can try iron sulphate (½ oz in a gallon of water per sq. yard) or a dilute solution of washing-up liquid but the real answer is to remove the turf and topsoil to a depth of 1 ft. The area of excavation should extend to 1 ft beyond the inner and outer edges of the ring, and all the earth should be moved well away from the lawn — take care not to spill any on the turf. Fill the hole with clean topsoil and then re-turf the area.

LICHEN

The leaf-like plates of lichen are a common sight on neglected lawns. The upper surface of each plate is brown or nearly black when moist, but when dry the surface fades to grey and curls upwards to reveal the white underside. Like moss, lichen is a clear indication of poor growing conditions — too little drainage, too much shade and too little food. The only place where you are likely to find lichen in a well-managed lawn is under trees.

Avoiding and curing the problem
Eradication is easy — apply dicophen to the affected area or treat the whole lawn with Lawn Sand at 2 oz per 10 sq. ft. Re-invasion, however, can only be prevented by improving the growing conditions. Spiking and the application of a lawn fertilizer are top priority operations. Liming is sometimes recommended for lichen control, but this should never be done unless a soil test has revealed extreme acidity — see page 46.

ALGAE

Green or black slime is sometimes found as a coating on the turf. This slime is made up of countless microscopic plants (blue-green algae) and is a feature of a bare or sparsely-grassed surface coupled with waterlogged conditions. It commonly occurs under the drip-line of trees, but you will also find it in turf on heavy soil which has been overrolled, underfed and cut too closely. It also attacks newly-seeded areas on badly drained soil.

Avoiding and curing the problem
Removing algal growth is quite a simple job — just water the affected area with dicophen. Routine treatment with Lawn Sand will also kill algae. Unfortunately the slime will return unless you can correct the basic cause. This calls for spiking and top dressing the compacted turf in autumn — see pages 35 and 44.

Weeds

A weed is a plant growing in the wrong place, and in the lawn that means any plant which is not a variety of grass recommended for turf production.

It is not unusual to see a newly-sown lawn infested with a wide variety of common weeds. When the lawn is established, however, the introduction of regular mowing brings about a spectacular change in the weed population. Most types cannot stand up to the destructive action of the whirling blades and so they steadily disappear. Many of the hard-to-kill nuisances of the flower border, such as couch grass, ground elder, bindweed and nettle are unable to exist in the cared-for lawn.

There remains a small group with a low-growing habit which enables them to escape the mower blades. These are the **lawn weeds**, which pose a constant threat to your turf. A few, such as annual meadow grass and parsley piert, are annuals but the vast majority are perennials which grow and spread each year.

There is nothing you can do to prevent occasional weeds from appearing in even the best cared-for lawn. Wind-borne and bird-borne seeds will see to that. But Nature cannot be blamed for the existence of large weed patches all over the turf. The basic reasons for this trouble are

- poor preparation of the site at lawn-making time
- poor choice of turf
- neglect or incorrect management

If your lawn is infested with weeds, you are to blame.

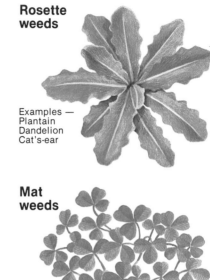

Rosette weeds

Examples —
Plantain
Dandelion
Cat's-ear

Mat weeds

Examples —
Pearlwort
Yarrow
Clover

WHERE THEY COME FROM

Bird-borne seeds. Droppings frequently contain weed seeds

Seeds and pieces of stem on lawn clippings — always use a grass box if the lawn is weedy

Wind-borne seeds from surrounding lawns

Creeping stems from surrounding weedy paths or neighbouring lawns

Bits of stem, root or seeds brought in on boots, compost, pets etc.

Seeds already in the soil. Bare patches or sparse growth can stimulate germination years after the making of a lawn. Deeply buried seeds can be brought to the surface by worms

WHY THEY MUST GO

Unsightly flowers — the lawn is given a distinctly spotty look

Unsightly leaves — the lawn becomes obviously second rate. The patchy appearance is heightened during a prolonged dry spell

Large leaves shade out and crowd out fine grasses

Roots take up water and nutrients, which reduces the reserves available for the grass. In this way lawn deterioration is accelerated

The mat-type weeds and the rosette weeds which produce runners can spread rapidly when the grass is not growing vigorously

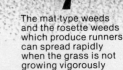

Avoiding the weed problem

1 WHEN MAKING THE LAWN, FALLOW THE SITE BEFORE SOWING SEED IN THE AUTUMN

Fallowing means the cultivation of the dug but unsown site at intervals during the summer. Each raking brings a new crop of annual weed seeds to the surface, where they germinate. These seedlings must then be destroyed before they flower — you can kill them by hoeing or you can use a 'chemical hoe' such as paraquat/diquat or glyphosate. Fallowing will ensure that the new grass will not be swamped by annual weeds.

2 WHEN MAKING THE LAWN, CHOOSE GOOD QUALITY SEED OR TURF

Buy seed from a reputable supplier. Remember that 'bargain' grass is often the most expensive in the long run. Good quality grass seed is carefully checked for purity before sale. There is no doubt that the seedsman is only rarely responsible for the weeds which come up with the grass — failure to fallow the land before sowing is a much more likely cause.

Poor quality turf is more usual than poor grade seed. Ask to see a sample before purchase — never buy badly infested material. Before laying, carefully inspect the turves and remove all weeds.

3 ON THE ESTABLISHED LAWN, BUILD UP RESISTANCE TO WEEDS BY GOOD MANAGEMENT

A thick growth of healthy grass will protect your lawn from a serious invasion by weeds. They need bare patches of earth or areas of slow-growing sparse grass in which to take hold and spread — your answer must be to ensure that these footholds are not provided. This calls for proper turf management as described in Chapter 3, and from all of these cultural rules there are six key points:

● **PROPER MOWING** Keep to the cutting heights and cutting frequencies set out on page 31. Cutting below these heights or cutting to the correct height at infrequent intervals will weaken the grass and let in weeds. Setting the blades as low as possible in order to shave off the weeds is foolish in the extreme. This 'little and often' rule for cutting grass is even more important on the new lawn than on established sites.

● **PROPER WATERING** If you fail to water the lawn during a prolonged dry spell then you will certainly save mowing time, but at some future date you may have to make up for it with extra weeding time. Once the rains return the weeds (including moss) will find a perfect breeding ground in the thin open turf produced by a severe drought.

● **PROPER SCARIFYING** Raking the turf helps to control creeping weeds and it also improves the vigour of the grass by penetrating the thatch which forms on the surface. But you must not overdo it — over-drastic raking can thin out the turf and let in weeds.

● **PROPER FEEDING** The role of feeding in weed control is to stimulate grass growth, which means that the spaces in which seeds can germinate are reduced or eliminated. Furthermore, high fertility helps the grass to compete for space against encroaching weeds.

● **PROPER WORM CONTROL** Worms add to the weed problem in two ways. Dormant weed seeds buried in the soil are brought to the surface, and the worm casts make ideal seed beds for those seeds and others which alight on the little heaps of bare earth. For details of worm control, see page 48.

● **PROPER DISEASE CONTROL** The usual result of a disease attack is a patch of weakened or dead grass, and this can be colonised by weeds or moss. Try to prevent disease attacks (see page 50) and if you are unfortunate enough to have a dead patch in the lawn, re-seed or re-turf before the weeds take over.

4 ON THE ESTABLISHED LAWN, CONTROL THE OCCASIONAL INVADER BY HAND WEEDING OR USING A WEEDKILLER

Hand weeding or spot treatment of individual weeds with a chemical may be all that is necessary. If weeds appear to be getting established you will need an overall treatment. Read the various ways of curing the problem on pages 54-57 and use the appropriate treatment.

Solving the weed problem

If the lawn has only a few weeds you may be tempted to ignore the problem — from a distance the turf appears uniformly green and only on closer inspection do the weeds become apparent. But the problem won't go away. The visual effect gets worse as the weeds start to flower, and these intruders will steadily increase their hold.

The problem should be tackled before it gets out of hand. There are both mechanical and chemical control methods — the right one to use depends on the number and types of weeds which are present. After the lawn has been freed from its unwelcome visitors, the rules of proper lawn care must be followed to increase the vigour of the grass and thereby reduce the chance of re-invasion. Chemical weed control is not a substitute for good management — it is just one of its important features.

MECHANICAL METHODS	CHEMICAL METHODS
HAND WEEDING Scattered seedlings of annual weeds can be removed quite simply from the newly-seeded lawn. Hold down the grass with one hand and pull out the weed with the other. In the established lawn this technique of hand pulling will not do — the weed has to be dug out. Choose a day when the turf is actively growing. Use a hand fork or a knife and make sure you dig out the root. Keep the diameter of the hole as narrow as possible and fill it with compost when the weed has been removed. Firm down the surrounding turf. Hand weeding is only practical for isolated weeds. **SLASHING** Clumps of coarse grass do not respond to lawn weedkillers. The recommended control method is to slash through the weed with a knife or edging iron before mowing. **RAKING UP** Before mowing rake upright the runners of creeping weeds, the stems of coarse grasses and the leaves of other weeds. In this way these stems and leaves will be cut off by the mower. Use the grass box on a weedy lawn and do not use the clippings for mulching around plants.	Your local shop or garden centre probably stocks a bewildering array of lawn weedkillers. The active ingredient or ingredients are stated on the front of the bottle, box or bag and these names reveal the type of weedkiller the package contains. If ferrous sulphate is named on the container, then the product is a *Lawn Sand* — if it contains other ingredients then it is a *selective weedkiller*. **LAWN SAND** **page 55** **SELECTIVE WEEDKILLER** **pages 56–57** The next three pages explain the nature of both of these two groups of lawn weedkillers, and their methods of use and modes of action do differ. There are, however, some general rules which apply to *all* weedkillers which are used on the lawn: ● Read both the instructions and precautions carefully before use . . . and do follow them. ● Put on the right amount — doubling the dose can scorch the grass and may actually decrease the weedkilling effect. A mechanical distributor is the most accurate method. ● The soil should be moist at the time of treatment and both the grass and weeds should be actively growing. This means that late spring or early summer is the best time for treatment. ● Do not treat the lawn when rain threatens or during a prolonged dry spell. ● Do not mow just before treatment. ● Store all weedkillers in a safe place when not in use.

Which method to use

TYPE OF WEED		METHOD OF CONTROL	
	BROAD-LEAVED WEEDS pages 59–77 'Broad-leaved' is a botanical rather than a descriptive term. A few of these weeds (e.g. pearlwort) have very narrow leaves	**LAWN SAND See page 55**	Destruction or reduction of the top growth of many weeds *plus* moss control *plus* green-up of lawn grasses
		— or —	
		SELECTIVE WEEDKILLER See pages 56–57	Destruction or reduction of both top growth and roots of many weeds. More effective than Lawn Sand, but there is no effect on moss
	MOSS page 78	**LAWN SAND See page 55**	Destruction or reduction of the top growth — moss will return if basic cause or causes are not removed
		— or —	
		MOSS KILLER	Specific moss killers based on dichlorophen are now available — see page 78
	WEED GRASSES page 79	**MECHANICAL CONTROL**	No satisfactory chemical control method is available. The appropriate mechanical control method depends on the type of weed grass present

LAWN SAND

The modern selective weedkillers have become extremely popular and old-fashioned Lawn Sand is now often ignored in the weedkiller programme. It is true that the active ingredient (ferrous sulphate) can scorch fine grasses when carelessly applied and it only kills the top growth and not the roots. But a wide variety of weeds, including moss, are kept in check. There is also the bonus from its other ingredient (ammonium sulphate) which gives the lawn a rich green colour and helps to maintain the acidic condition which is so vital.

The dividing line between Lawn Sand and selective weedkillers is no longer clear cut. Numerous lawn weedkillers now contain the active ingredients of both types.

The way to use it

Sunny morning with the prospect of fine weather

Even application by hand or applicator is vital.

Do not overdose, but the lawn can be treated several times during the season

Grass moist with dew

Soil must be moist at time of treatment. Do not use during drought

After using Lawn Sand

Immediately following treatment:	Do not mow or walk on the lawn until rain has fallen or until it has been watered.
2 days later:	Thoroughly water the lawn if rain has not fallen since application.
3 weeks later:	Rake up dead undergrowth. If clumps of weeds are still present, use a selective weedkiller (see pages 56–57) or apply a further dressing of Lawn Sand.

How it works

Powder clings to the rough, broad leaves of weeds. Rapid scorch and leaf destruction result

Powder slides off the narrow, smooth leaves of fine grasses. Temporary blackening of older grass leaves often occurs, but rapid recovery of the grasses takes place once the powder has been washed off the leaves

Powder is washed off the leaves and into the soil by rain or by watering. The grass-stimulating and colour-enriching effect then occurs

When to use it

Treatment Period				
APRIL	MAY	JUNE	JULY	AUG

Best time for treatment

For autumn moss control, use dichlorophen (see page 78). For autumn weed control, use a liquid selective weedkiller (see page 56)

The effect of Lawn Sand

Untreated   **Treated**

SELECTIVE WEEDKILLER

Treatment with Lawn Sand will not control plantains and buttercups in your lawn — it was the discovery of MCPA and 2,4-D which provided the answer. These were the first 'hormone' weedkillers, developed in Britain and the U.S. during World War II. They are not true hormones (the correct name is 'plant growth-regulating substances') and the products they contain are now referred to as systemic, translocated or selective weedkillers. These chemicals have become basic tools for the care of the lawn. Their main blessing is that they are selective in their action — killing susceptible weeds but sparing resistant plants (such as grasses) when used at the recommended rate. They work inside the weed, killing the roots as well as the leaves.

Unfortunately the early selective weedkillers had a limited range — they were not very effective against clovers, pearlwort, yarrow etc., but today there are newer ones which can control these weeds.

WHICH TYPE OF PRODUCT TO CHOOSE

POWDER or GRANULAR SELECTIVE WEEDKILLER *plus* FERTILIZER

The most popular way of weeding and feeding the lawn at the same time — there is no doubt that a selective weedkiller works better when a nitrogen-rich fertilizer is used with it. Some experts feel that a fertilizer applied 1–2 weeks *before* weedkiller treatment is more effective as active growth will then start earlier.

LIQUID SELECTIVE WEEDKILLER

The quickest-acting way of killing weeds in the lawn. The golden rule is to *always* add a soluble fertilizer when you are treating the whole lawn and *never* add a fertilizer when you are treating patches of weeds. Several liquid weedkiller/fertilizer mixtures are available.

SPOT or WAX BAR SELECTIVE WEEDKILLER

Scattered rosette weeds can be spot-treated with a pinch of a powder weedkiller, but there are special products available for spot treatment. Weed guns and aerosols are squirted into the heart of the weed — wax bars are stroked over the leaves. Expensive if there are many weeds to treat.

WHAT TO LOOK FOR ON THE LABEL

The names of the selective weedkiller ingredients will be on the front of the pack. The day of the product which contained only MCPA or 2,4-D is over. The weedkiller you buy should preferably contain an ingredient from each of the two groups listed below:

GROUP 1 The early ones MCPA 2,4-D	Effective against cat's-ear, hawkweed, plantains, buttercups, docks and dandelion. Slow-acting, and repeat treatment is necessary with many weed types. Some important weeds are resistant.
GROUP 2 The later ones DICAMBA DICHLORPROP MECOPROP	Effective against many of the weeds which are resistant or moderately resistant to MCPA or 2,4-D. Examples are yarrow, knotgrass, selfheal, clovers and pearlwort. Not quite as safe to fine grasses as the early ones so take care not to overdose.

Many products these days have a double or triple action due to the presence of additional ingredients. Moss will be controlled if dichlorophen or ferrous sulphate is listed and there will be a greening-up effect if some form of nitrogen is included. The trace elements magnesium and iron may also be listed.

The label should state that the product is for home garden use. It is illegal for gardeners to use pesticides labelled for farmers or professional growers.

The effect of selective weedkiller+fertilizer

Untreated   **Treated**

The way to use it

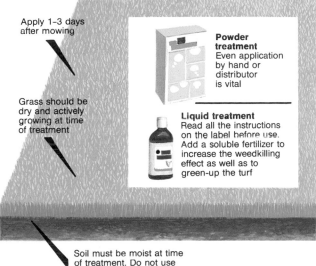

A warm and still day with the prospect of fine weather. Windy conditions lead to drift and damage to garden plants — heavy rain shortly after treatment can neutralise the effect

Apply 1–3 days after mowing

Grass should be dry and actively growing at time of treatment

Powder treatment
Even application by hand or distributor is vital

Liquid treatment
Read all the instructions on the label before use. Add a soluble fertilizer to increase the weedkilling effect as well as to green-up the turf

Soil must be moist at time of treatment. Do not use during drought

After using a selective weedkiller

Wait at least 3 days before cutting again. Most weeds should be killed by a single application, but with others a second treatment may be necessary about 6 weeks later.

SAFETY TO PEOPLE, PETS AND PLANTS

The old word 'hormone' is unfortunate — these weedkillers are not true hormones and certainly do not have any hormone-like effect on man and animals. They will not harm adults or children, pets or wildlife when used as directed. Take the standard precautions you would with any pesticide — keep away from fish and do not have pets on the lawn while you are treating it. After you've finished wash hands and face.

Garden plants are much more sensitive than animals because the product cannot distinguish between a susceptible weed and a susceptible garden shrub or flower. So it is up to you to protect them — keep a special watering can or sprayer just for weedkillers and wash out everything thoroughly after use. Avoid drift on to beds or borders and pay special attention near a greenhouse. After use store the bottle, box or bag well away from plants — never in the greenhouse.

METHODS OF APPLICATION

With liquid weedkillers, the most effective method of application is a knapsack sprayer but the tiny droplets produced are liable to drift. So don't use a sprayer on a small lawn surrounded by shrubs and flowers — use a watering can fitted with a fine rose or weeder bar.

With powder or granular weedkillers, a fertilizer distributor (see page 36) is the best method. Avoid missed strips and overlapping — a blue-coloured product will help to show where you have been. Hand application is used for small areas and is quite acceptable, but do spread a measured dose evenly over a small marked-out area before you begin. Note the cover obtained — then treat the rest of the lawn with a similar coating.

How it works

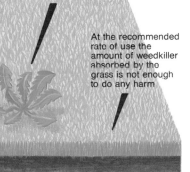

The hormone fraction is absorbed by the leaves and rapidly passes to all parts of the weed. If it is a susceptible variety, growth is stimulated at first, and pronounced twisting and curling of the leaves takes place. The foliage usually stands much more upright than normal and then the weed finally dies and the leaves rot away.

There is no rapid scorching effect and this may disappoint the new gardener. Control may take place in 2–6 weeks, but the great advantage is that the whole plant and not just the foliage is affected

At the recommended rate of use the amount of weedkiller absorbed by the grass is not enough to do any harm

When to use it

Treatment Period					
APRIL	MAY	JUNE	JULY	AUG	SEPT

Best time for treatment

For September treatment, use a liquid selective weedkiller *without* incorporating a nitrogen-rich fertilizer.

NEW LAWNS AND RE-SEEDING

Wait twelve months after sowing seed or six months after laying turf before applying a selective weedkiller which is not specially made for new lawns. After treatment of an established lawn, bare patches may appear once large clumps of weeds have died down — re-seeding can take place six weeks after treatment.

BULBS IN THE LAWN

Treatment can take place when the leaves of the bulbs have completely withered. Late summer is a good time for this work.

DISPOSAL OF CLIPPINGS

Lawn clippings obtained shortly after treatment can be used for making compost by the Recycler method — see page 101. Do not use clippings for mulch around plants until the lawn has been mown at least four times following weedkiller application.

The WEED INDEX

Out of the hundreds of weed species which infest gardens in this country, only a handful — about 20 at the most — are common lawn weeds. It is a good idea to have a working knowledge of these important types because if one of them really takes hold then it can rapidly colonise a large area. The following pages will show you how to identify the common and not-so-common lawn weeds, and also how to control them.

DOCKS & SORRELS

The two common docks which infest our gardens — the curled dock and the broad-leaved dock — can be a nuisance in the newly-sown lawn, so do try to get rid of the roots when preparing the seed bed. Fortunately these large-leaved weeds rarely survive in the regularly-mown lawn, but the smaller docks, known as sorrels, produce enough low-growing foliage to enable the plants to withstand mowing. This means that the sorrels are true lawn weeds.

Sheep's sorrel can be a serious nuisance but its close relative, the common sorrel, is much less frequent in turf. They will only thrive in acid conditions but liming is not the answer. Use a weedkiller and feed regularly to control them.

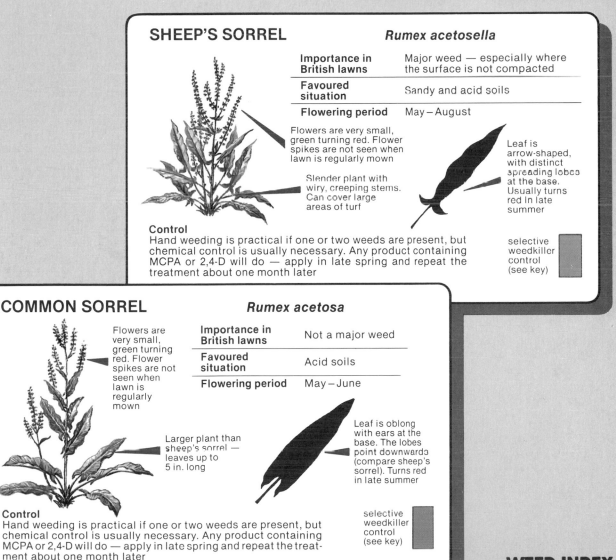

SHEEP'S SORREL   *Rumex acetosella*

Importance in British lawns	Major weed — especially where the surface is not compacted
Favoured situation	Sandy and acid soils
Flowering period	May – August

Flowers are very small, green turning red. Flower spikes are not seen when lawn is regularly mown

Slender plant with wiry, creeping stems. Can cover large areas of turf

Leaf is arrow-shaped, with distinct spreading lobes at the base. Usually turns red in late summer

Control
Hand weeding is practical if one or two weeds are present, but chemical control is usually necessary. Any product containing MCPA or 2,4-D will do — apply in late spring and repeat the treatment about one month later

selective weedkiller control (see key)

COMMON SORREL   *Rumex acetosa*

Flowers are very small, green turning red. Flower spikes are not seen when lawn is regularly mown

Importance in British lawns	Not a major weed
Favoured situation	Acid soils
Flowering period	May – June

Larger plant than sheep's sorrel — leaves up to 5 in. long

Leaf is oblong with ears at the base. The lobes point downwards (compare sheep's sorrel). Turns red in late summer

Control
Hand weeding is practical if one or two weeds are present, but chemical control is usually necessary. Any product containing MCPA or 2,4-D will do — apply in late spring and repeat the treatment about one month later

selective weedkiller control (see key)

WEED INDEX

The BUTTERCUPS

Buttercups are part of the lawn scene — pretty yellow flowers dotted about the turf when mowing is delayed for one reason or another. The most common type is creeping buttercup and you will see it everywhere — the one you are least likely to see is lesser celandine, which will thrive only under damp and shady conditions.

For some lawn owners the occasional buttercup is not regarded as offensive, but the problem is that creeping buttercup can cover a large area of turf at an alarming rate. Fortunately this weed is sensitive to all the selective weedkiller products, so control is very easy. The other common buttercups pose more of a problem, but control is never really difficult.

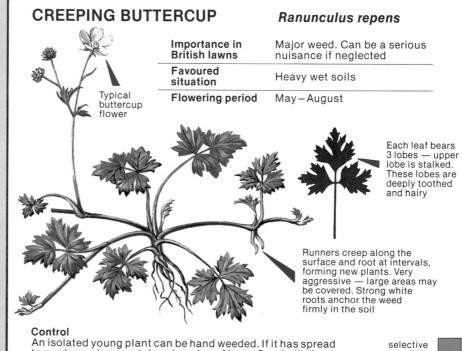

CREEPING BUTTERCUP — *Ranunculus repens*

Importance in British lawns	Major weed. Can be a serious nuisance if neglected
Favoured situation	Heavy wet soils
Flowering period	May – August

Typical buttercup flower

Each leaf bears 3 lobes — upper lobe is stalked. These lobes are deeply toothed and hairy

Runners creep along the surface and root at intervals, forming new plants. Very aggressive — large areas may be covered. Strong white roots anchor the weed firmly in the soil

Control

An isolated young plant can be hand weeded. If it has spread to produce a large patch, a dressing of Lawn Sand will check its growth. The best method by far, however, is to use a selective weedkiller — any product containing MCPA or 2,4-D will kill this weed

selective weedkiller control (see key)

CHEMICAL CONTROL KEY

Weed consistently killed by one application

Weed may be killed by one application, but a second treatment is often necessary

Weed checked by one application, but repeat treatments will be necessary

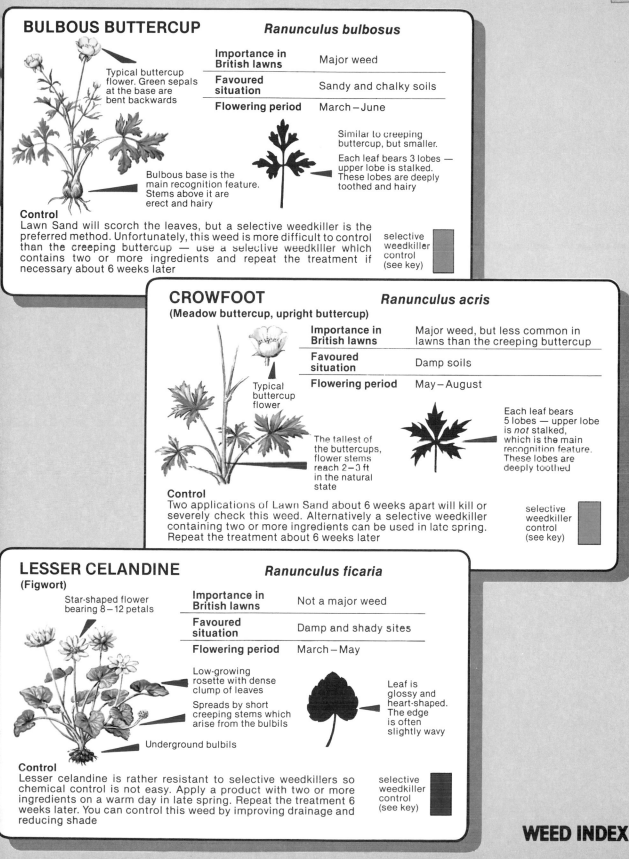

BULBOUS BUTTERCUP
Ranunculus bulbosus

Typical buttercup flower. Green sepals at the base are bent backwards

Importance in British lawns	Major weed
Favoured situation	Sandy and chalky soils
Flowering period	March – June

Similar to creeping buttercup, but smaller.

Each leaf bears 3 lobes — upper lobe is stalked. These lobes are deeply toothed and hairy

Bulbous base is the main recognition feature. Stems above it are erect and hairy

Control
Lawn Sand will scorch the leaves, but a selective weedkiller is the preferred method. Unfortunately, this weed is more difficult to control than the creeping buttercup — use a selective weedkiller which contains two or more ingredients and repeat the treatment if necessary about 6 weeks later

selective weedkiller control (see key)

CROWFOOT
Ranunculus acris
(Meadow buttercup, upright buttercup)

Importance in British lawns	Major weed, but less common in lawns than the creeping buttercup
Favoured situation	Damp soils
Flowering period	May – August

Typical buttercup flower

The tallest of the buttercups, flower stems reach 2 – 3 ft in the natural state

Each leaf bears 5 lobes — upper lobe is *not* stalked, which is the main recognition feature. These lobes are deeply toothed

Control
Two applications of Lawn Sand about 6 weeks apart will kill or severely check this weed. Alternatively a selective weedkiller containing two or more ingredients can be used in late spring. Repeat the treatment about 6 weeks later

selective weedkiller control (see key)

LESSER CELANDINE
Ranunculus ficaria
(Figwort)

Star-shaped flower bearing 8 – 12 petals

Importance in British lawns	Not a major weed
Favoured situation	Damp and shady sites
Flowering period	March – May

Low-growing rosette with dense clump of leaves

Spreads by short creeping stems which arise from the bulbils

Underground bulbils

Leaf is glossy and heart-shaped. The edge is often slightly wavy

Control
Lesser celandine is rather resistant to selective weedkillers so chemical control is not easy. Apply a product with two or more ingredients on a warm day in late spring. Repeat the treatment 6 weeks later. You can control this weed by improving drainage and reducing shade

selective weedkiller control (see key)

WEED INDEX

The PLANTAINS

Plantains occur everywhere — from the large, broad-leaved rosettes which infest neglected turf to the clumps of starweed which bedevil carefully-tended seaside golf courses. Recognition of the plantains is simple — clusters of leathery and prominently-ribbed leaves with erect spikes of tiny flowers. The width of the leaves varies with the type of plantain — the largest leaves belong to greater plantain, the most serious weed in this group.

Eradication is no problem. Hand weeding is practical for the occasional invader, and a single treatment with a selective weedkiller should be enough to get rid of a more widespread attack.

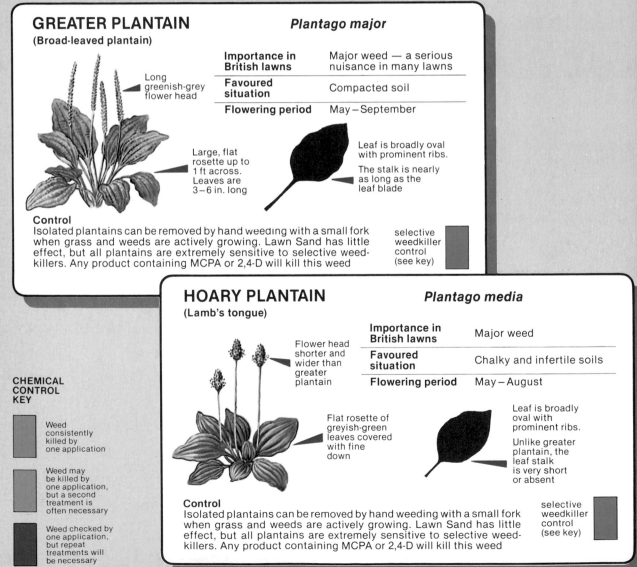

GREATER PLANTAIN
(Broad-leaved plantain)

Plantago major

Long greenish-grey flower head

Importance in British lawns	Major weed — a serious nuisance in many lawns
Favoured situation	Compacted soil
Flowering period	May – September

Large, flat rosette up to 1 ft across. Leaves are 3–6 in. long

Leaf is broadly oval with prominent ribs.

The stalk is nearly as long as the leaf blade

Control
Isolated plantains can be removed by hand weeding with a small fork when grass and weeds are actively growing. Lawn Sand has little effect, but all plantains are extremely sensitive to selective weed-killers. Any product containing MCPA or 2,4-D will kill this weed

selective weedkiller control (see key)

HOARY PLANTAIN
(Lamb's tongue)

Plantago media

Flower head shorter and wider than greater plantain

Importance in British lawns	Major weed
Favoured situation	Chalky and infertile soils
Flowering period	May – August

Flat rosette of greyish-green leaves covered with fine down

Leaf is broadly oval with prominent ribs.

Unlike greater plantain, the leaf stalk is very short or absent

Control
Isolated plantains can be removed by hand weeding with a small fork when grass and weeds are actively growing. Lawn Sand has little effect, but all plantains are extremely sensitive to selective weed-killers. Any product containing MCPA or 2,4-D will kill this weed

selective weedkiller control (see key)

CHEMICAL CONTROL KEY

Weed consistently killed by one application

Weed may be killed by one application, but a second treatment is often necessary

Weed checked by one application, but repeat treatments will be necessary

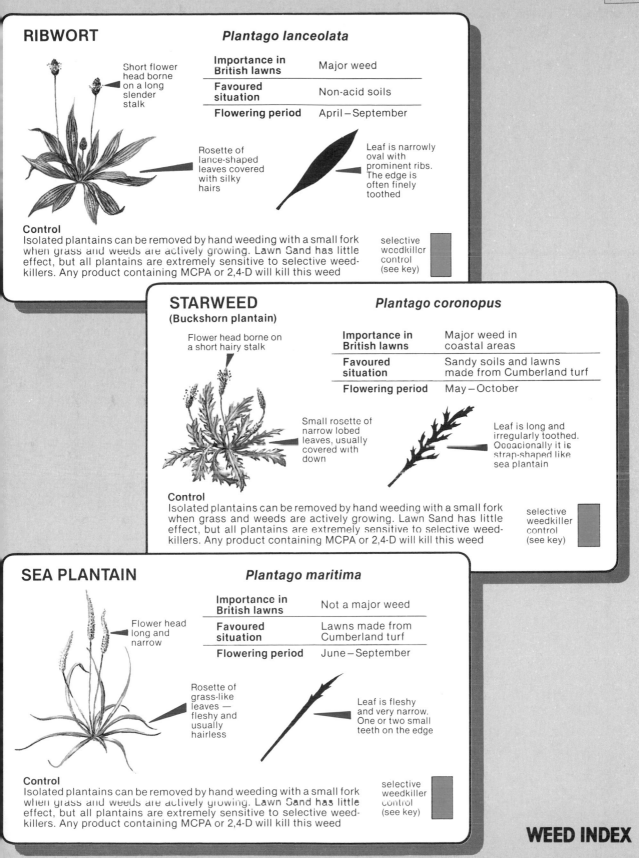

RIBWORT

Plantago lanceolata

Short flower head borne on a long slender stalk

Importance in British lawns	Major weed
Favoured situation	Non-acid soils
Flowering period	April – September

Rosette of lance-shaped leaves covered with silky hairs

Leaf is narrowly oval with prominent ribs. The edge is often finely toothed

Control
Isolated plantains can be removed by hand weeding with a small fork when grass and weeds are actively growing. Lawn Sand has little effect, but all plantains are extremely sensitive to selective weed-killers. Any product containing MCPA or 2,4-D will kill this weed

selective weedkiller control (see key)

STARWEED
(Buckshorn plantain)

Plantago coronopus

Flower head borne on a short hairy stalk

Importance in British lawns	Major weed in coastal areas
Favoured situation	Sandy soils and lawns made from Cumberland turf
Flowering period	May – October

Small rosette of narrow lobed leaves, usually covered with down

Leaf is long and irregularly toothed. Occasionally it is strap-shaped like sea plantain

Control
Isolated plantains can be removed by hand weeding with a small fork when grass and weeds are actively growing. Lawn Sand has little effect, but all plantains are extremely sensitive to selective weed-killers. Any product containing MCPA or 2,4-D will kill this weed

selective weedkiller control (see key)

SEA PLANTAIN

Plantago maritima

Flower head long and narrow

Importance in British lawns	Not a major weed
Favoured situation	Lawns made from Cumberland turf
Flowering period	June – September

Rosette of grass-like leaves — fleshy and usually hairless

Leaf is fleshy and very narrow. One or two small teeth on the edge

Control
Isolated plantains can be removed by hand weeding with a small fork when grass and weeds are actively growing. Lawn Sand has little effect, but all plantains are extremely sensitive to selective weed-killers. Any product containing MCPA or 2,4-D will kill this weed

selective weedkiller control (see key)

WEED INDEX

The CLOVERS

Clover is a major headache for many lawn owners. During the dry days of midsummer the bright green patches stand out against the dull and pale grass. This patchy effect is an eyesore, and control was difficult until the discovery of the newer-type selective weedkillers described on page 56.

The clovers you are most likely to see are white clover and the smaller yellow-flowering species known as lesser trefoil. As with all clovers, they are encouraged by both water shortage and nitrogen shortage. So wherever clover is a problem you should feed with a nitrogen-rich fertilizer every spring — never use a phosphate- or potash-rich fertilizer at the start of the season.

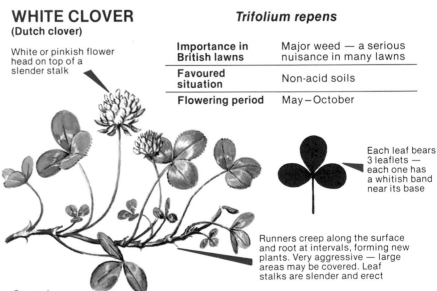

WHITE CLOVER
(Dutch clover)

Trifolium repens

White or pinkish flower head on top of a slender stalk

Importance in British lawns	Major weed — a serious nuisance in many lawns
Favoured situation	Non-acid soils
Flowering period	May–October

Each leaf bears 3 leaflets — each one has a whitish band near its base

Runners creep along the surface and root at intervals, forming new plants. Very aggressive — large areas may be covered. Leaf stalks are slender and erect

Control
If clover has become well-established use a combination of techniques. Rake regularly before mowing so that the creeping stems are brought up to meet the blades. Also water the lawn during drought, or clover will spread rapidly. In addition a chemical attack is needed. Lawn Sand is a useful treatment in spring — top growth is burnt off and vital nitrogen for clover control is provided. Apply a selective weedkiller which contains two or more ingredients in June or July — repeat the treatment 6 weeks later

selective weedkiller control (see key)

CHEMICAL CONTROL KEY

Weed consistently killed by one application

Weed may be killed by one application, but a second treatment is often necessary

Weed checked by one application, but repeat treatments will be necessary

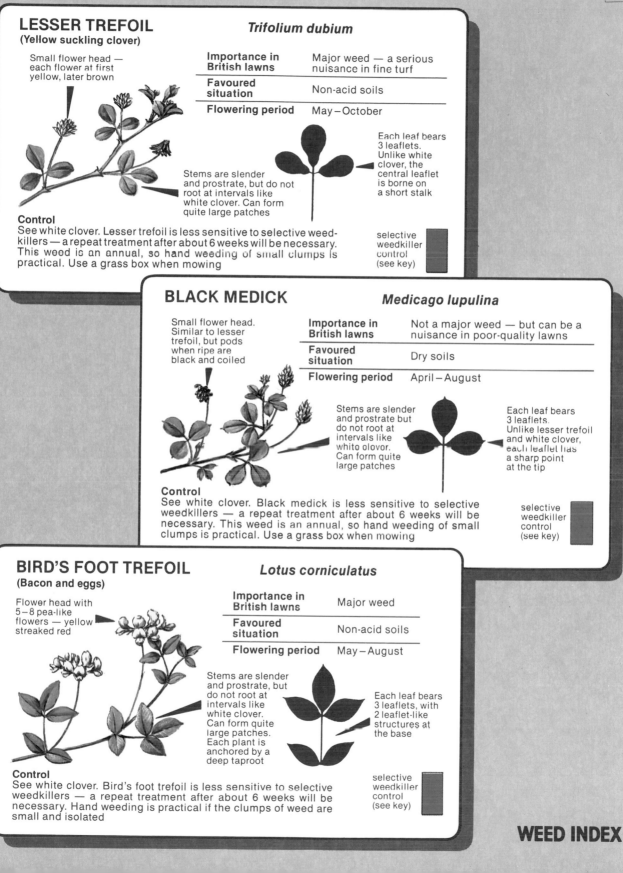

LESSER TREFOIL
(Yellow suckling clover)

Trifolium dubium

Small flower head — each flower at first yellow, later brown

Importance in British lawns	Major weed — a serious nuisance in fine turf
Favoured situation	Non-acid soils
Flowering period	May – October

Each leaf bears 3 leaflets. Unlike white clover, the central leaflet is borne on a short stalk

Stems are slender and prostrate, but do not root at intervals like white clover. Can form quite large patches

Control
See white clover. Lesser trefoil is less sensitive to selective weed-killers — a repeat treatment after about 6 weeks will be necessary. This weed is an annual, so hand weeding of small clumps is practical. Use a grass box when mowing

selective weedkiller control (see key)

BLACK MEDICK

Medicago lupulina

Small flower head. Similar to lesser trefoil, but pods when ripe are black and coiled

Importance in British lawns	Not a major weed — but can be a nuisance in poor-quality lawns
Favoured situation	Dry soils
Flowering period	April – August

Stems are slender and prostrate but do not root at intervals like white clover. Can form quite large patches

Each leaf bears 3 leaflets. Unlike lesser trefoil and white clover, each leaflet has a sharp point at the tip

Control
See white clover. Black medick is less sensitive to selective weedkillers — a repeat treatment after about 6 weeks will be necessary. This weed is an annual, so hand weeding of small clumps is practical. Use a grass box when mowing

selective weedkiller control (see key)

BIRD'S FOOT TREFOIL
(Bacon and eggs)

Lotus corniculatus

Flower head with 5–8 pea-like flowers — yellow streaked red

Importance in British lawns	Major weed
Favoured situation	Non-acid soils
Flowering period	May – August

Stems are slender and prostrate, but do not root at intervals like white clover. Can form quite large patches. Each plant is anchored by a deep taproot

Each leaf bears 3 leaflets, with 2 leaflet-like structures at the base

Control
See white clover. Bird's foot trefoil is less sensitive to selective weedkillers — a repeat treatment after about 6 weeks will be necessary. Hand weeding is practical if the clumps of weed are small and isolated

selective weedkiller control (see key)

WEED INDEX

The DANDELION-LIKE WEEDS

The dandelion-like weeds can be very disfiguring, their large leaves forming distinct rosettes which bear the all-too-familiar yellow flower heads. The chances are the invaders in your lawn are either the true dandelion or cat's-ear, for these are the only really common ones. The remainder are occasional nuisances, and the autumn hawkbit is uncommon.

Fortunately, all these weeds can be controlled by one or two applications of a modern selective weed-killer. Choose a day in spring when the weeds are actively growing.

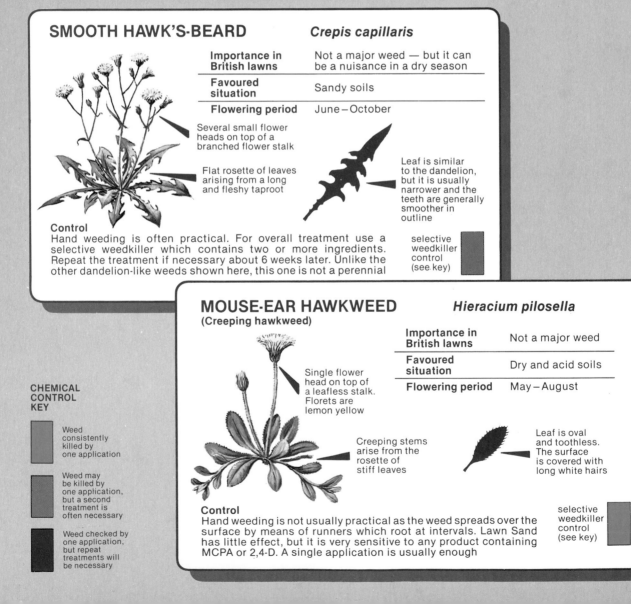

SMOOTH HAWK'S-BEARD   *Crepis capillaris*

Importance in British lawns	Not a major weed — but it can be a nuisance in a dry season
Favoured situation	Sandy soils
Flowering period	June – October

Several small flower heads on top of a branched flower stalk

Flat rosette of leaves arising from a long and fleshy taproot

Leaf is similar to the dandelion, but it is usually narrower and the teeth are generally smoother in outline

Control
Hand weeding is often practical. For overall treatment use a selective weedkiller which contains two or more ingredients. Repeat the treatment if necessary about 6 weeks later. Unlike the other dandelion-like weeds shown here, this one is not a perennial

selective weedkiller control (see key)

MOUSE-EAR HAWKWEED
(Creeping hawkweed)   *Hieracium pilosella*

Importance in British lawns	Not a major weed
Favoured situation	Dry and acid soils
Flowering period	May – August

Single flower head on top of a leafless stalk. Florets are lemon yellow

Creeping stems arise from the rosette of stiff leaves

Leaf is oval and toothless. The surface is covered with long white hairs

Control
Hand weeding is not usually practical as the weed spreads over the surface by means of runners which root at intervals. Lawn Sand has little effect, but it is very sensitive to any product containing MCPA or 2,4-D. A single application is usually enough

selective weedkiller control (see key)

CHEMICAL CONTROL KEY

Weed consistently killed by one application

Weed may be killed by one application, but a second treatment is often necessary

Weed checked by one application, but repeat treatments will be necessary

AUTUMN HAWKBIT *Leontodon autumnalis*

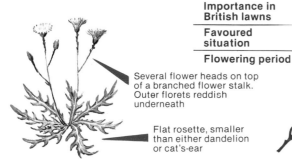

Importance in British lawns	Uncommon
Favoured situation	Badly drained soils
Flowering period	July — October

Several flower heads on top of a branched flower stalk. Outer florets reddish underneath

Flat rosette, smaller than either dandelion or cat's-ear

Leaf is narrow, pointed and very deeply toothed. Surface is shiny and hairless

Control
Hand weeding is possible, but any bit of root remaining in the soil will produce a new plant. Chemical spot treatment is better — for overall treatment use a selective weedkiller which contains two or more ingredients. Repeat the treatment if necessary about 6 weeks later. Lawn Sand has very little effect

selective weedkiller control (see key)

DANDELION *Taraxacum officinale*

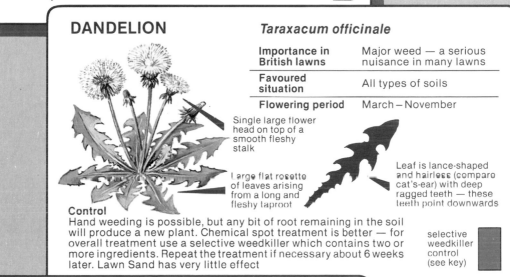

Importance in British lawns	Major weed — a serious nuisance in many lawns
Favoured situation	All types of soils
Flowering period	March — November

Single large flower head on top of a smooth fleshy stalk

Large flat rosette of leaves arising from a long and fleshy taproot

Leaf is lance-shaped and hairless (compare cat's-ear) with deep ragged teeth — these teeth point downwards

Control
Hand weeding is possible, but any bit of root remaining in the soil will produce a new plant. Chemical spot treatment is better — for overall treatment use a selective weedkiller which contains two or more ingredients. Repeat the treatment if necessary about 6 weeks later. Lawn Sand has very little effect

selective weedkiller control (see key)

CAT'S-EAR *Hypochaeris radicata*

Importance in British lawns	Major weed — a serious nuisance in many lawns
Favoured situation	All types of soils
Flowering period	May — September

One or two dandelion-like heads on top of a flower stalk bearing tiny black scale leaves

Flat rosette of leaves arising from a long and fleshy taproot

Leaf is lance-shaped and toothed like a dandelion, but it is hairy, fleshy and the teeth do not point downwards

Control
Hand weeding is possible, but any bit of root remaining in the soil will produce a new plant. Chemical spot treatment is better — for overall treatment use a selective weedkiller which contains two or more ingredients. Repeat the treatment if necessary about 6 weeks later

selective weedkiller control (see key)

WEED INDEX

The SPEEDWELLS

Speedwells are small plants with pretty blue flowers, and a number of our native species occasionally appear in turf. The thyme-leaved, wall and field speedwells are rare, but the germander speedwell is a nuisance in many areas. The only speedwell which is a serious lawn weed is not a wild flower at all — the slender speedwell is a garden escape, having been introduced in the 19th century. It spreads not by seed but by bits of stem scattered during mowing. Until quite recently the selective weedkiller ioxynil was used to control the speedwells but this chemical is no longer available. Unfortunately the other selective weedkillers are less effective, even when repeat applications are made.

SLENDER SPEEDWELL
(Round-leaved speedwell)
Veronica filiformis

Small mauve-coloured flower on top of a thread-like stalk. Rarely produces seed

Importance in British lawns	Major weed — increasing in importance in many areas
Favoured situation	Damp soils
Flowering period	April — June

Stems are slender and prostrate, rooting at intervals to form new plants. Can form large patches

Leaf is round or kidney-shaped. Edge is ruffled

Control
Hand weeding is only practical if a few plants are present. Where a large area is affected Lawn Sand will help to keep it in check if applied in spring. Control with a selective weedkiller is difficult — use a product containing dicamba or mecoprop and apply repeat treatment

selective weedkiller control (see key)

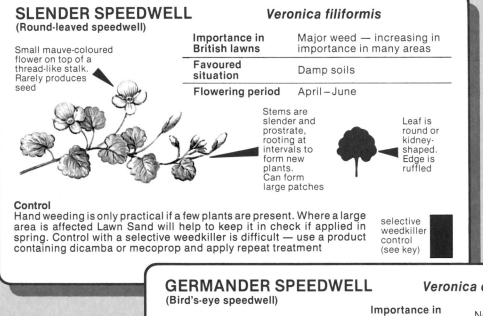

GERMANDER SPEEDWELL
(Bird's-eye speedwell)
Veronica chamaedrys

Small blue-coloured flower with a white eye

Importance in British lawns	Not a major weed
Favoured situation	Damp soils
Flowering period	April — June

Stems are slender and prostrate, rooting at intervals to form new plants. Can form large patches

Leaf is oval and coarsely toothed. The leaf-stalk is short or absent

Control
Hand weeding is only practical if a few plants are present. Where a large area is affected Lawn Sand will help to keep it in check if applied in spring. Control with a selective weedkiller is difficult — use a product containing dicamba or mecoprop and apply repeat treatment

selective weedkiller control (see key)

CHEMICAL CONTROL KEY

Weed consistently killed by one application

Weed may be killed by one application, but a second treatment is often necessary

Weed checked by one application, but repeat treatments will be necessary

The CHICKWEEDS

Chickweed can be a problem in the flower and vegetable garden — growing and spreading everywhere unless we hoe, spray or hand pull the pale-green straggling stems. However, common chickweed cannot stand regular mowing, so it rarely occurs in the established lawn. But it has a close relative, the common mouse-ear chickweed, which is not killed by the mower. This weed can spread at an alarming rate, especially if the soil is chalky and dry. The answer is to treat the silvery patches as soon as they begin to appear. Fortunately it is susceptible to the newer chemicals used in modern lawn weedkillers.

COMMON MOUSE-EAR CHICKWEED *Cerastium holosteoides*

Small white flowers appear in clusters on top of erect flowering stem

Dense cluster of creeping stems with prostrate leaves. The weed appears silvery. A large spreading mat can be formed

Leaf is oval and hairy

Importance in British lawns	Major weed
Favoured situation	All soils
Flowering period	April — September

Control
This weed is severely checked by a spring dressing of Lawn Sand, but a selective weedkiller containing dicamba or mecoprop is the best answer. A single treatment when the weed and grass are growing actively should be sufficient to control it

selective weedkiller control (see key)

COMMON CHICKWEED   *Stellaria media*

Small white flowers with 5 deeply-divided petals. Stamens are deep red

Weak straggling stems form a tangled mat. Each stem bears a single vertical line of hairs

Leaf is heart-shaped and stalked

Importance in British lawns	Not important in established lawns
Favoured situation	Newly-sown lawns
Flowering period	February — November

Control
Regular mowing will generally eradicate this weed once the lawn is established. If it persists, use a selective weedkiller containing dicamba or mecoprop. A single treatment when the weed and grass are growing actively should be sufficient to control it

selective weedkiller control (see key)

WEED INDEX

The THISTLES

Thistles bedevil the farmer and many gardeners, but they are not usually troublesome on the lawn. Very few can survive constant mowing, and although the commonest species (creeping thistle) can be serious in a new lawn it gradually succumbs to regular mowing. Just one species can thrive below the cutter blades — the dwarf thistle which produces a rosette of leaves and bears its flowers in the heart of the plant.

Hand weeding or spot treatment is the way to deal with isolated thistles, but an overall spray with a modern selective weedkiller is the most effective method if a large area is involved. Lawn Sand is ineffective against thistles.

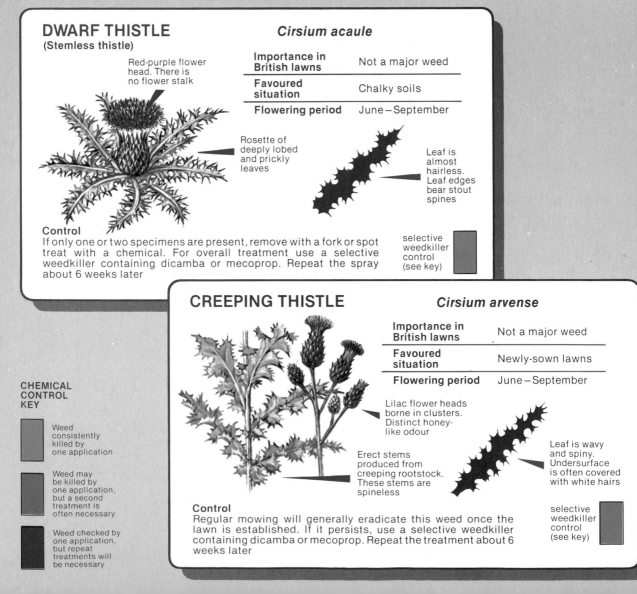

DWARF THISTLE
(Stemless thistle)

Cirsium acaule

Red-purple flower head. There is no flower stalk

Importance in British lawns	Not a major weed
Favoured situation	Chalky soils
Flowering period	June – September

Rosette of deeply lobed and prickly leaves

Leaf is almost hairless. Leaf edges bear stout spines

Control
If only one or two specimens are present, remove with a fork or spot treat with a chemical. For overall treatment use a selective weedkiller containing dicamba or mecoprop. Repeat the spray about 6 weeks later

selective weedkiller control (see key)

CREEPING THISTLE

Cirsium arvense

Importance in British lawns	Not a major weed
Favoured situation	Newly-sown lawns
Flowering period	June – September

Lilac flower heads borne in clusters. Distinct honey-like odour

Erect stems produced from creeping rootstock. These stems are spineless

Leaf is wavy and spiny. Undersurface is often covered with white hairs

Control
Regular mowing will generally eradicate this weed once the lawn is established. If it persists, use a selective weedkiller containing dicamba or mecoprop. Repeat the treatment about 6 weeks later

selective weedkiller control (see key)

CHEMICAL CONTROL KEY

Weed consistently killed by one application

Weed may be killed by one application, but a second treatment is often necessary

Weed checked by one application, but repeat treatments will be necessary

DAISY & PEARLWORT

Daisies and pearlwort look nothing like each other, yet they do have a number of features in common. They occur in all soil types, and their favourite site is compacted turf which is mown very closely. Obviously, raising the height of cut, regular feeding and spiking will check their spread, but if large clumps are present a chemical treatment is necessary. Both are susceptible to modern weedkillers, but their main feature in common is that many gardeners do not object to them — daisies for the children to pick, pearlwort to add a grass-like greenness to the lawn. But beware — they both can quickly spread and destroy large areas of grass.

DAISY

Bellis perennis

Flower needs little description — white ray florets with bright yellow centre. Closes at night, hence old name 'day's-eye'

Importance in British lawns	Major weed — especially in closely-mown turf
Favoured situation	All soils
Flowering period	March – November

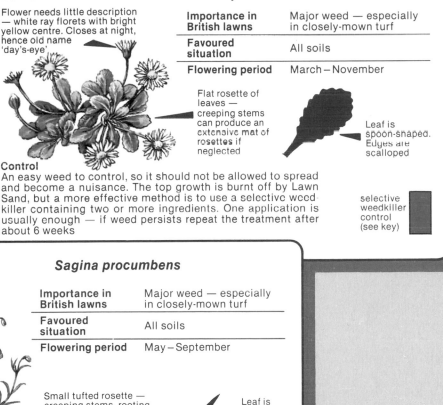

Flat rosette of leaves — creeping stems can produce an extensive mat of rosettes if neglected

Leaf is spoon-shaped. Edges are scalloped

Control
An easy weed to control, so it should not be allowed to spread and become a nuisance. The top growth is burnt off by Lawn Sand, but a more effective method is to use a selective weed-killer containing two or more ingredients. One application is usually enough — if weed persists repeat the treatment after about 6 weeks

selective weedkiller control (see key)

PEARLWORT
(Procumbent pearlwort)

Sagina procumbens

Tiny flower on top of a thin stalk. White petals may or may not be present

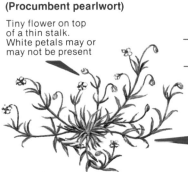

Importance in British lawns	Major weed — especially in closely-mown turf
Favoured situation	All soils
Flowering period	May – September

Small tufted rosette — creeping stems, rooting at intervals, spread out from the rosette to form a dense mat of weed

Leaf is small and narrow

Control
An easy weed to control, so it should not be allowed to spread and become a nuisance. The top growth is burnt off by Lawn Sand, but a more effective method is to use a selective weedkiller containing two or more ingredients. One application will be enough, but pearlwort will soon return unless you feed the grass and avoid mowing too closely

selective weedkiller control (see key)

WEED INDEX

YARROW & WOODRUSH

Although these two weeds are not related they do form a close association in many lawns. Both thrive where the soil is sandy and when it is low in nitrogen and humus — they are good indicators of a lawn in poor condition. Another link is their resistance to weedkillers — yarrow is easier to kill than woodrush but both require more than one treatment to ensure good control and it will take more than one season to eradicate them if they have been left to get out of hand. Modern weedkillers are a great help, but these weeds will return if the turf is not improved by feeding each spring and top dressing each autumn.

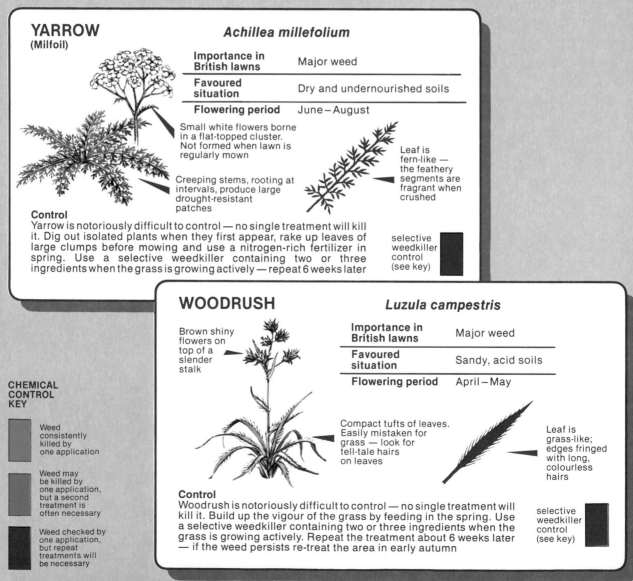

YARROW
(Milfoil)

Achillea millefolium

Importance in British lawns	Major weed
Favoured situation	Dry and undernourished soils
Flowering period	June – August

Small white flowers borne in a flat-topped cluster. Not formed when lawn is regularly mown

Leaf is fern-like — the feathery segments are fragrant when crushed

Creeping stems, rooting at intervals, produce large drought-resistant patches

Control
Yarrow is notoriously difficult to control — no single treatment will kill it. Dig out isolated plants when they first appear, rake up leaves of large clumps before mowing and use a nitrogen-rich fertilizer in spring. Use a selective weedkiller containing two or three ingredients when the grass is growing actively — repeat 6 weeks later

selective weedkiller control (see key)

WOODRUSH

Luzula campestris

Brown shiny flowers on top of a slender stalk

Importance in British lawns	Major weed
Favoured situation	Sandy, acid soils
Flowering period	April – May

Compact tufts of leaves. Easily mistaken for grass — look for tell-tale hairs on leaves

Leaf is grass-like; edges fringed with long, colourless hairs

Control
Woodrush is notoriously difficult to control — no single treatment will kill it. Build up the vigour of the grass by feeding in the spring. Use a selective weedkiller containing two or three ingredients when the grass is growing actively. Repeat the treatment about 6 weeks later — if the weed persists re-treat the area in early autumn

selective weedkiller control (see key)

CHEMICAL CONTROL KEY

Weed consistently killed by one application

Weed may be killed by one application, but a second treatment is often necessary

Weed checked by one application, but repeat treatments will be necessary

SELFHEAL & PARSLEY-PIERT

These two are grouped together because they are both common lawn weeds which are often ignored but can spread rapidly and cover large patches of turf. Apart from their importance they have nothing else in common. Selfheal is a perennial which infests heavy land — parsley-piert is an annual which invades light, impoverished soils. Parsley-piert can be a serious problem in closely-mown turf as its myriads of seeds are produced all season long and will colonise any bare patch which is available. As with so many weed problems, the answer is to use chemical control coupled with better management to prevent re-invasion.

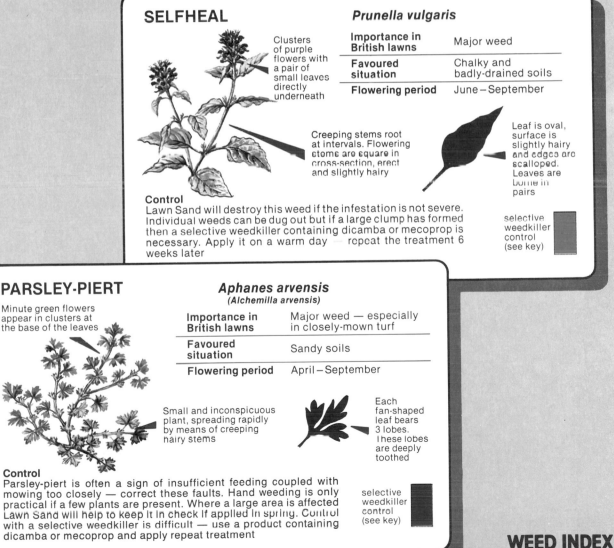

SELFHEAL   *Prunella vulgaris*

Clusters of purple flowers with a pair of small leaves directly underneath

Importance in British lawns	Major weed
Favoured situation	Chalky and badly-drained soils
Flowering period	June – September

Creeping stems root at intervals. Flowering stems are square in cross-section, erect and slightly hairy

Leaf is oval, surface is slightly hairy and edges are scalloped. Leaves are borne in pairs

Control
Lawn Sand will destroy this weed if the infestation is not severe. Individual weeds can be dug out but if a large clump has formed then a selective weedkiller containing dicamba or mecoprop is necessary. Apply it on a warm day — repeat the treatment 6 weeks later

selective weedkiller control (see key)

PARSLEY-PIERT   *Aphanes arvensis*
(*Alchemilla arvensis*)

Minute green flowers appear in clusters at the base of the leaves

Importance in British lawns	Major weed — especially in closely-mown turf
Favoured situation	Sandy soils
Flowering period	April – September

Small and inconspicuous plant, spreading rapidly by means of creeping hairy stems

Each fan-shaped leaf bears 3 lobes. These lobes are deeply toothed

Control
Parsley-piert is often a sign of insufficient feeding coupled with mowing too closely — correct these faults. Hand weeding is only practical if a few plants are present. Where a large area is affected Lawn Sand will help to keep it in check if applied in spring. Control with a selective weedkiller is difficult — use a product containing dicamba or mecoprop and apply repeat treatment

selective weedkiller control (see key)

WEED INDEX

OTHER LAWN WEEDS

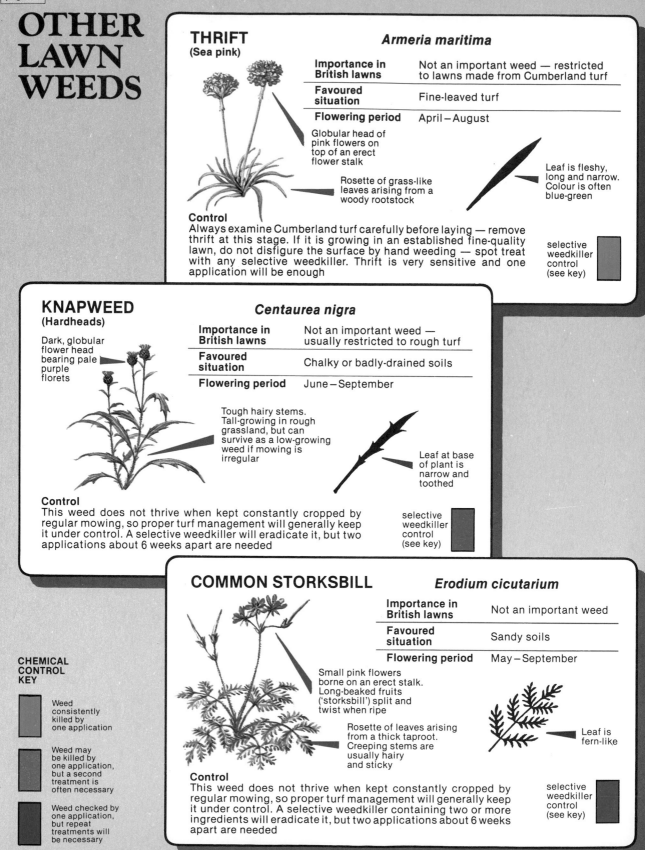

THRIFT
(Sea pink)
Armeria maritima

Importance in British lawns	Not an important weed — restricted to lawns made from Cumberland turf
Favoured situation	Fine-leaved turf
Flowering period	April — August

Globular head of pink flowers on top of an erect flower stalk

Rosette of grass-like leaves arising from a woody rootstock

Leaf is fleshy, long and narrow. Colour is often blue-green

Control
Always examine Cumberland turf carefully before laying — remove thrift at this stage. If it is growing in an established fine-quality lawn, do not disfigure the surface by hand weeding — spot treat with any selective weedkiller. Thrift is very sensitive and one application will be enough

selective weedkiller control (see key)

KNAPWEED
(Hardheads)
Centaurea nigra

Dark, globular flower head bearing pale purple florets

Importance in British lawns	Not an important weed — usually restricted to rough turf
Favoured situation	Chalky or badly-drained soils
Flowering period	June — September

Tough hairy stems. Tall-growing in rough grassland, but can survive as a low-growing weed if mowing is irregular

Leaf at base of plant is narrow and toothed

Control
This weed does not thrive when kept constantly cropped by regular mowing, so proper turf management will generally keep it under control. A selective weedkiller will eradicate it, but two applications about 6 weeks apart are needed

selective weedkiller control (see key)

COMMON STORKSBILL
Erodium cicutarium

Importance in British lawns	Not an important weed
Favoured situation	Sandy soils
Flowering period	May — September

Small pink flowers borne on an erect stalk. Long-beaked fruits ('storksbill') split and twist when ripe

Rosette of leaves arising from a thick taproot. Creeping stems are usually hairy and sticky

Leaf is fern-like

Control
This weed does not thrive when kept constantly cropped by regular mowing, so proper turf management will generally keep it under control. A selective weedkiller containing two or more ingredients will eradicate it, but two applications about 6 weeks apart are needed

selective weedkiller control (see key)

CHEMICAL CONTROL KEY

Weed consistently killed by one application

Weed may be killed by one application, but a second treatment is often necessary

Weed checked by one application, but repeat treatments will be necessary

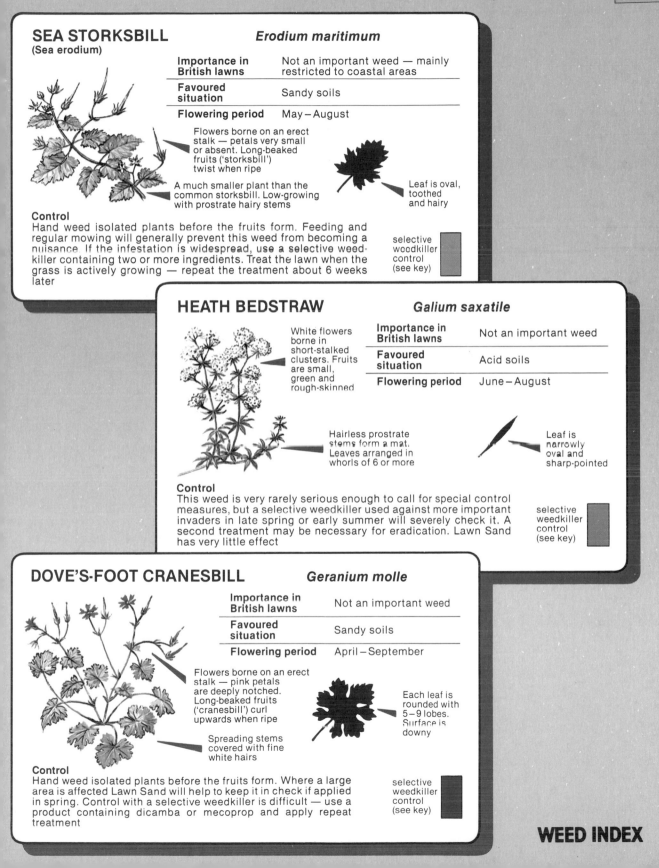

SEA STORKSBILL
(Sea erodium)

Erodium maritimum

Importance in British lawns	Not an important weed — mainly restricted to coastal areas
Favoured situation	Sandy soils
Flowering period	May – August

Flowers borne on an erect stalk — petals very small or absent. Long-beaked fruits ('storksbill') twist when ripe

A much smaller plant than the common storksbill. Low-growing with prostrate hairy stems

Leaf is oval, toothed and hairy

Control
Hand weed isolated plants before the fruits form. Feeding and regular mowing will generally prevent this weed from becoming a nuisance. If the infestation is widespread, use a selective weedkiller containing two or more ingredients. Treat the lawn when the grass is actively growing — repeat the treatment about 6 weeks later

selective weedkiller control (see key)

HEATH BEDSTRAW

Galium saxatile

White flowers borne in short-stalked clusters. Fruits are small, green and rough-skinned

Importance in British lawns	Not an important weed
Favoured situation	Acid soils
Flowering period	June – August

Hairless prostrate stems form a mat. Leaves arranged in whorls of 6 or more

Leaf is narrowly oval and sharp-pointed

Control
This weed is very rarely serious enough to call for special control measures, but a selective weedkiller used against more important invaders in late spring or early summer will severely check it. A second treatment may be necessary for eradication. Lawn Sand has very little effect

selective weedkiller control (see key)

DOVE'S-FOOT CRANESBILL

Geranium molle

Importance in British lawns	Not an important weed
Favoured situation	Sandy soils
Flowering period	April – September

Flowers borne on an erect stalk — pink petals are deeply notched. Long-beaked fruits ('cranesbill') curl upwards when ripe

Each leaf is rounded with 5–9 lobes. Surface is downy

Spreading stems covered with fine white hairs

Control
Hand weed isolated plants before the fruits form. Where a large area is affected Lawn Sand will help to keep it in check if applied in spring. Control with a selective weedkiller is difficult — use a product containing dicamba or mecoprop and apply repeat treatment

selective weedkiller control (see key)

WEED INDEX

OTHER LAWN WEEDS continued

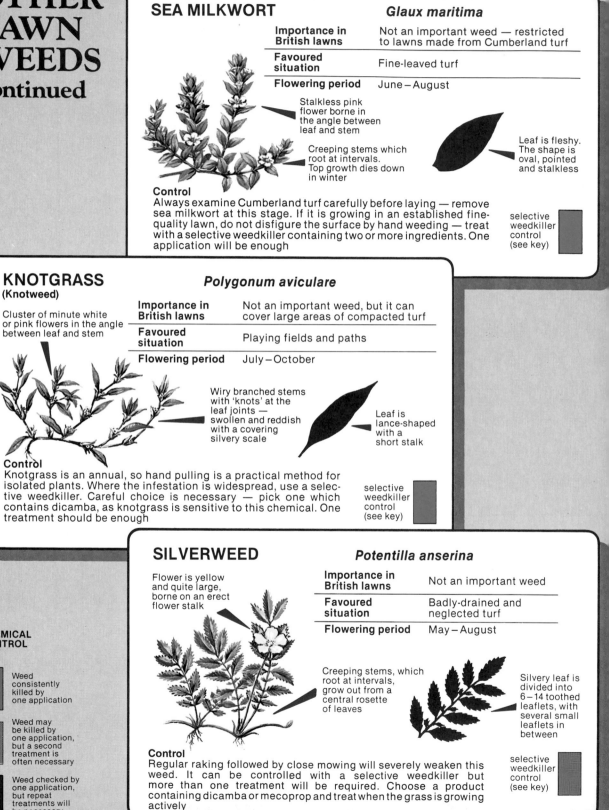

SEA MILKWORT — *Glaux maritima*

Importance in British lawns	Not an important weed — restricted to lawns made from Cumberland turf
Favoured situation	Fine-leaved turf
Flowering period	June – August

Stalkless pink flower borne in the angle between leaf and stem

Creeping stems which root at intervals. Top growth dies down in winter

Leaf is fleshy. The shape is oval, pointed and stalkless

Control
Always examine Cumberland turf carefully before laying — remove sea milkwort at this stage. If it is growing in an established fine-quality lawn, do not disfigure the surface by hand weeding — treat with a selective weedkiller containing two or more ingredients. One application will be enough

selective weedkiller control (see key)

KNOTGRASS (Knotweed) — *Polygonum aviculare*

Importance in British lawns	Not an important weed, but it can cover large areas of compacted turf
Favoured situation	Playing fields and paths
Flowering period	July – October

Cluster of minute white or pink flowers in the angle between leaf and stem

Wiry branched stems with 'knots' at the leaf joints — swollen and reddish with a covering silvery scale

Leaf is lance-shaped with a short stalk

Control
Knotgrass is an annual, so hand pulling is a practical method for isolated plants. Where the infestation is widespread, use a selective weedkiller. Careful choice is necessary — pick one which contains dicamba, as knotgrass is sensitive to this chemical. One treatment should be enough

selective weedkiller control (see key)

SILVERWEED — *Potentilla anserina*

Importance in British lawns	Not an important weed
Favoured situation	Badly-drained and neglected turf
Flowering period	May – August

Flower is yellow and quite large, borne on an erect flower stalk

Creeping stems, which root at intervals, grow out from a central rosette of leaves

Silvery leaf is divided into 6 – 14 toothed leaflets, with several small leaflets in between

Control
Regular raking followed by close mowing will severely weaken this weed. It can be controlled with a selective weedkiller but more than one treatment will be required. Choose a product containing dicamba or mecoprop and treat when the grass is growing actively

selective weedkiller control (see key)

CHEMICAL CONTROL KEY

Weed consistently killed by one application

Weed may be killed by one application, but a second treatment is often necessary

Weed checked by one application, but repeat treatments will be necessary

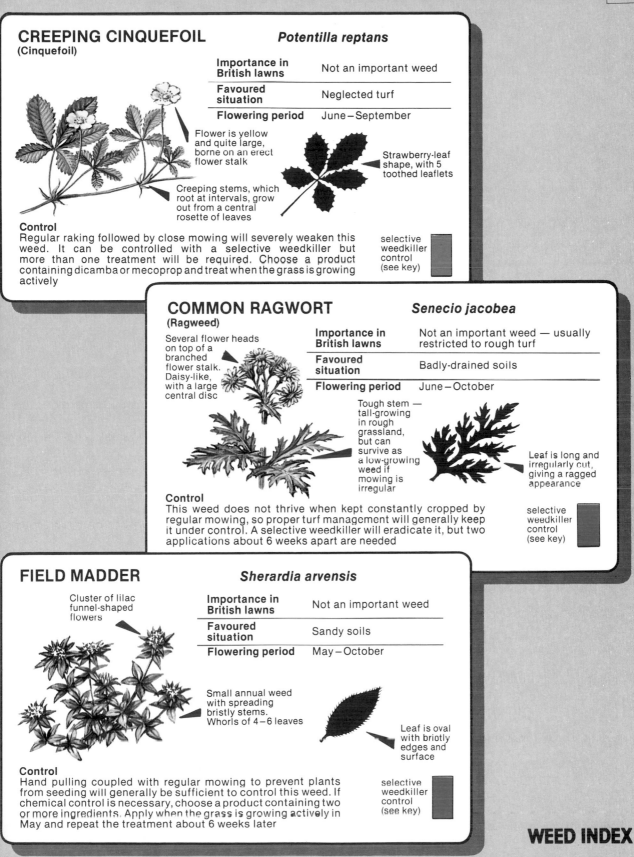

CREEPING CINQUEFOIL
(Cinquefoil)

Potentilla reptans

Importance in British lawns	Not an important weed
Favoured situation	Neglected turf
Flowering period	June – September

Flower is yellow and quite large, borne on an erect flower stalk

Strawberry-leaf shape, with 5 toothed leaflets

Creeping stems, which root at intervals, grow out from a central rosette of leaves

Control
Regular raking followed by close mowing will severely weaken this weed. It can be controlled with a selective weedkiller but more than one treatment will be required. Choose a product containing dicamba or mecoprop and treat when the grass is growing actively

selective weedkiller control (see key)

COMMON RAGWORT
(Ragweed)

Senecio jacobea

Several flower heads on top of a branched flower stalk. Daisy-like, with a large central disc

Importance in British lawns	Not an important weed — usually restricted to rough turf
Favoured situation	Badly-drained soils
Flowering period	June – October

Tough stem — tall-growing in rough grassland, but can survive as a low-growing weed if mowing is irregular

Leaf is long and irregularly cut, giving a ragged appearance

Control
This weed does not thrive when kept constantly cropped by regular mowing, so proper turf management will generally keep it under control. A selective weedkiller will eradicate it, but two applications about 6 weeks apart are needed

selective weedkiller control (see key)

FIELD MADDER

Sherardia arvensis

Cluster of lilac funnel-shaped flowers

Importance in British lawns	Not an important weed
Favoured situation	Sandy soils
Flowering period	May – October

Small annual weed with spreading bristly stems. Whorls of 4–6 leaves

Leaf is oval with bristly edges and surface

Control
Hand pulling coupled with regular mowing to prevent plants from seeding will generally be sufficient to control this weed. If chemical control is necessary, choose a product containing two or more ingredients. Apply when the grass is growing actively in May and repeat the treatment about 6 weeks later

selective weedkiller control (see key)

WEED INDEX

MOSS

Moss is a tiny non-flowering plant and yet it is for many gardeners the worst of all lawn troubles. The basic point you must realise is that moss is a symptom and not the primary cause of run-down turf. This means that just using a moss killer is not enough — the only way to ensure permanent freedom from moss is to find the cause or causes and correct them.

Dampness is essential for the spread of mosses, so spring and autumn are the main periods of rapid colonisation in lawns which have one or more high-risk factors such as compaction coupled with poor drainage. Waterlogged patches almost always develop moss.

But too much moisture is not the only high-risk factor — moss is a common sight on infertile sandy soils which drain very freely. Underfeeding can be the cause — so can overacidity, too much shade and cutting too closely. Less well known is drought as a high-risk factor — yet failure to water in the dry days of summer is a common cause of an autumn moss problem.

Large patches call for a moss eradication programme. Removal of the causes will result in the slow disappearance of the problem and the prevention of its return. Eradication can be greatly speeded up by the use of a moss-killing chemical. These work quickly, so large patches of bare earth may develop before the grass has had a chance to grow back. This is an open invitation for weeds, so re-seed or re-turf the bare spots once moss has gone.

UPRIGHT MOSSES

Upright tufts; green leaves at top, brown leaves at base

Symptom of dry, acid soil

TRAILING MOSSES

Green or golden feathery stems, prostrate on the surface

Symptom of shade or poor drainage

CUSHION MOSSES

Tiny upright stems closely packed together to form compact cushions

Symptom of mowing too closely

MOSS CONTROL

- **Apply a moss killer in spring.** You have two choices. Lawn Sand (see page 55) will burn out moss and also effectively provide a boost to grass growth. Alternatively you could use a dichlorophen product which is watered on to the affected area. After a couple of weeks rake out the dead moss and re-seed the bare patches.

- **Feed the lawn.** Regular feeding in spring or early summer is vital to keep the grass growing strongly — see page 36.

- **Cut at the correct height.** Shaving the lawn at less than the recommended height weakens the grass and is one of the main causes of moss in luxury lawns. Scalping the surface and leaving bare patches is even more likely to lead to moss invasion. Leaving the grass long is not the answer — over-long grass and damp weather can lead to colonisation by the trailing mosses. Cut at the *correct* height (see page 31) and use a grass box.

- **Reduce shade, if possible.** Removing lower branches may help, but moss is usually inevitable in grass growing under trees which form a dense cover.

- **Scarify and aerate the lawn.** Removal of the surface mat by raking and the improvement of drainage by spiking are important operations in the moss control programme.

- **Top dress the lawn.** Building up the fertility of the turf by top dressing in autumn is beneficial in the fight against moss, especially if the soil is sandy or shallow.

- **Lime, if necessary.** Overacidity can favour moss, but do not lime unless you are sure it is necessary (see page 46).

- **Apply a moss killer in autumn.** Use a dichlorophen product through a watering can or sprayer.

The WEED GRASSES

Broad-leaved plants are not the only weeds you will find in a lawn — there are a few species of native grasses which can be distinctly undesirable. These weed grasses have an extra drawback compared with their broad-leaved counterparts — there is no chemical treatment which can be used to kill them and yet spare the desirable lawn varieties.

There are two basic types of weed grasses. The first one consists of the coarse-leaved species which form unsightly clumps in closely-mown turf. The commonest example of these coarse grasses is yorkshire fog but there are others — cocksfoot, creeping soft grass and wall barley grass.

The second type is annual meadow grass. This low-growing species is almost universal in lawns and generally does not form unsightly clumps like the coarse grasses. It blends quite well with utility varieties of lawn grass and in some situations it is actually considered a desirable species — it will grow under trees or in heavily compacted areas where no other lawn grass could survive. But annual meadow grass can easily become a serious nuisance — if the turf is weak and sparse then this weed grass will rapidly colonise large areas or even the whole lawn, partly or completely replacing the lawn grasses. Then you have a problem, because this grass is susceptible to disease and drought, and is liable to discolour or die out in midsummer.

WEED GRASS CONTROL

- Take time to prepare a proper seed bed when making a new lawn. Follow the rules laid down in Chapter 7.

- Buy good quality seed. 'Bargain' mixtures may contain seeds of weed grasses as an impurity.

- Maintain vigorous grass growth throughout the season by feeding, aerating and watering the lawn as described in Chapter 3. Annual meadow grass is much less likely to invade your lawn if there are no bare patches to colonise.

- Worm casts make ideal seed beds for annual meadow grass. Chemicals for worm control are no longer available, so brushing away casts is the only answer.

- If you see an isolated patch of coarse grass or annual meadow grass, dig out the patch and then re-seed or re-turf.

- Where the patches of coarse grass are too numerous to make hand weeding practical, slash the weed grasses with a knife or edging iron before mowing.

- Rake up the grass foliage before mowing — change the direction of the cut each time you mow.

- If annual meadow grass is a problem, use a grass box.

COUCH GRASS IN THE LAWN

In beds and borders this weed grass can be a nightmare, but it is not a problem in the lawn. Remove roots and shoots of couch grass when preparing the ground for a new lawn, but do not worry if some couch appears amongst the grass seedlings. It will rapidly succumb to regular mowing and will die out in the first season.

YORKSHIRE FOG
Holcus lanatus

Leaves soft and woolly

ANNUAL MEADOW GRASS
Poa annua

Low-growing; leaves crinkled

Brown patches

Brown patches on the lawn can be due to any of a score of possible causes. It is easy for even the most experienced gardener to make a wrong diagnosis, but with the help of the table below you should be able, with reasonable accuracy, to track down the most probable cause of this trouble in your lawn.

SHAPE OF AFFECTED AREA	COLOUR OF AFFECTED AREA	TIME OF YEAR WHEN IT IS USUALLY SEEN	SPECIAL POINTS OF RECOGNITION	KEY QUESTION FOR IDENTIFICATION
Irregular patches or whole lawn	**Straw-coloured**	Late spring or summer	Soil below surface abnormally dry	"Did the brown patches occur after a prolonged period of dry weather?"
Circular or irregular patches, 1 in. to 1 ft in diameter	**Yellow or brown**	Autumn in damp weather	A white or pale pink mould appears on the affected area in damp weather	"Does a white mould develop on a piece of moist turf if kept in a jar for a few days?"
Irregular patches, spreading to 1 yard or more	**Straw-coloured, often distinctly pink**	Late summer or autumn	Tiny branched red needles projecting from the leaves of dead grass	"Are the patches large and do the affected grass stems bear small red hairs, which are jelly-like in wet weather?"
Circular patches, 1 – 2 in. in diameter	**Straw-coloured or brown**	Late summer in damp weather	Patches remain small and circular, although they may coalesce	"Are the patches small and is the grass Creeping Red Fescue?"
Irregular patches which may spread rapidly	**Brown**	Spring or early summer	Birds searching for grubs	"Can the brown grass be easily pulled away, and are legless grey or brown grubs present in the soil?"
Irregular patches, or regular stripes and curves where a distributor has been used	**Brown or black**	Spring or summer	Patches or stripes appear suddenly, a few days after application of fertilizer	'Was insufficient care paid to the even distribution of the fertilizer — was the recommended rate used?"
Roughly circular patches	**Brown**	Any time of the year	A ring of deep green grass surrounds each patch	"Does a bitch have access to the lawn?"
Irregular patch or patches	**Brown**	Spring, summer or autumn	Patches appear suddenly, a few days after mowing	"Has the mower been refuelled or oiled whilst standing on or near the affected area?"
Irregular patch or patches	**Yellow or brown**	Any time of the year	Lawn recently created on a site which contained rubble or other debris	"Were stones or bricks left in the soil before the area was seeded or turfed?"
Irregular patches or whole lawn	**Yellow or brown**	Any time of the year	Grass thin and sparse — moss frequently present. Top layer of soil compacted	"Is it impossible to push a matchstick completely into the moist turf by pressing it down with the ball of your thumb?"

THE TROUBLE MAKERS

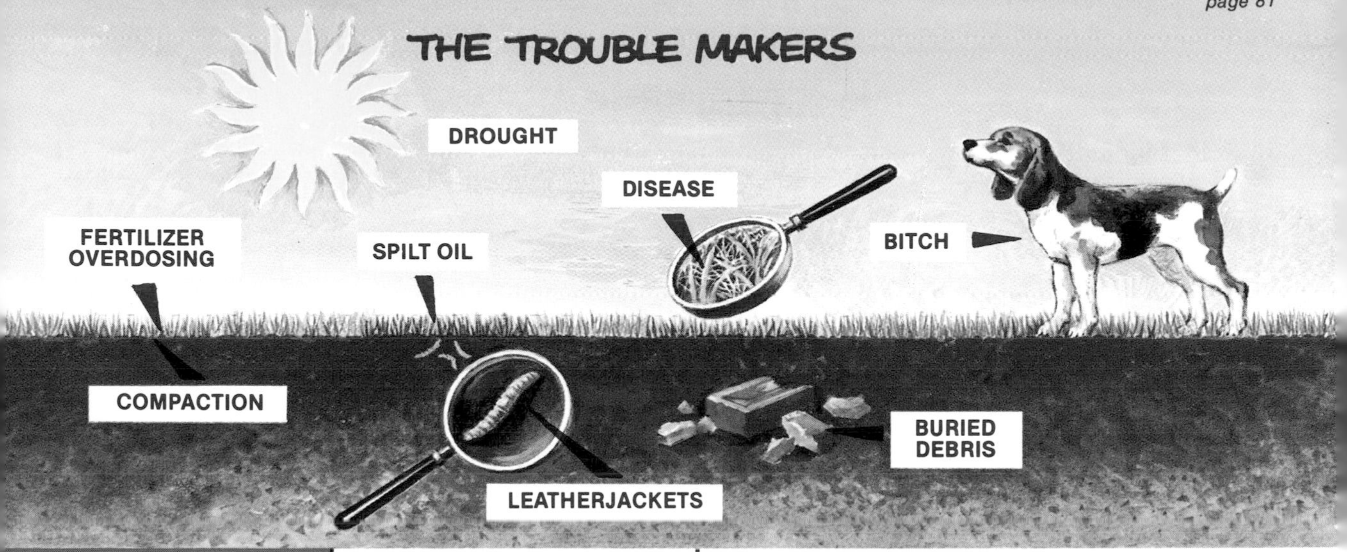

DROUGHT

DISEASE

FERTILIZER
OVERDOSING

SPILT OIL

BITCH

COMPACTION

LEATHERJACKETS

BURIED
DEBRIS

IF THE ANSWER IS YES – MOST PROBABLE CAUSE	AREAS WHERE TROUBLE IS MOST SERIOUS	CURE OR PREVENTION
Drought	Sandy areas	The lawn should be copiously watered during dry weather *before* discoloration occurs. If browning has already taken place, spike the surface and water thoroughly.
Fusarium patch disease	Poorly drained and shady areas	See page 50
Red thread disease	Sandy areas Luxury turf, especially when underfed	See page 50
Dollar spot disease	Luxury turf, especially when underfed	See page 50
Leatherjackets	Coastal areas Poorly drained turf	See page 48
Fertilizer overdosing	All areas	Always water in fertilizer if rain does not fall for two days after application. Use a liquid fertilizer if the weather is hot and dry. Whichever product you use, follow the maker's instructions.
Bitch urine	All areas	Water the affected area copiously — this will reduce but not eradicate the discoloration. Re-seeding the dead area may be necessary.
Spilt oil	All areas	Always move the mower off the lawn before oiling or refuelling.
Buried debris	All areas, especially new lawns	Lift back turf, remove offending object or objects and then add sufficient soil to level the surface. Replace turf and fill in cracks with sifted soil.
Compaction	Heavy soil areas	Aerate compacted turf in autumn (see page 44). Re-seed or re-turf the affected area. If waterlogging persists some form of drainage system may be necessary.

Lawn repairs

Bare patches, broken edges, bumps and hollows are all serious problems when they occur in a prominent area of the lawn. Together they make up the main cause of the patchy effect which spoils so many lawns, and they can make mowing more difficult than usual.

Poor soil preparation before laying turf or sowing seed will quickly lead to the need for repair work, but even the best-laid lawn will one day require a little surgery. Only a small amount of effort is required to ensure the removal of the eyesores listed on these two pages.

The secret is to pick the right time — this usually means when the trouble is first noticed. Even more important is to pick the right season (autumn is best, or April if this is not possible). The weather should be showery.

Much of this work involves using replacement pieces of turf or the re-seeding of small areas. The grasses making up the turf or seed should be similar to those present in the lawn. The best source of turf for this purpose is from a section of the lawn where its loss will hardly be noticed. The stripped area is then built up and re-seeded.

BROKEN EDGES

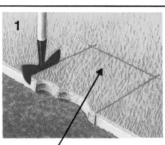

1 Cut out a square of turf carrying the broken edge. Prise it up gently with a spade to free it from the soil.

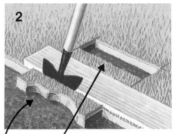

2 Move this turf forward so that the damaged part projects beyond the border.

Trim to line up with the rest of the lawn.

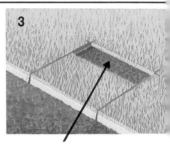

3 Fill up the gap with either turf or with soil which is then firmed and sown with grass seed. If turf is used, fill cracks with sifted soil.

BUMPS

Bumps are regularly scalped by the mower and therefore tend to become bare. Do not attempt to roll out bumps — this will generally make the area more unsightly than ever.

HOLLOWS

The most usual cause of a depression is either inadequate consolidation at lawn-making time or the rotting of organic material below the surface. Hollows drain more slowly than the rest of the lawn in wet weather. The grass is generally greener and lusher, and the risk of disease is increased. Small hollows can be gradually filled in by working sifted soil (no more than ½ in. thickness at a time) into the turf at regular intervals. Deep hollows call for surgery, as described on the right.

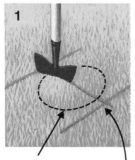

1 Area of bump or hollow.

Cut turf with a spade or edging iron. Peel back the turves carefully.

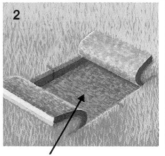

2 Remove or add soil as necessary to level the turf. If the bump is prominent and the soil is shallow, remove some subsoil and replace topsoil. Tread down the disturbed soil.

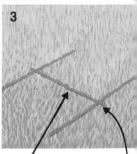

3 Firm down the rolled-back turf after checking that the area is level.

Fill cracks with sifted soil.

BARE PATCHES

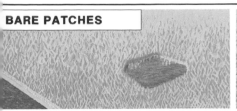

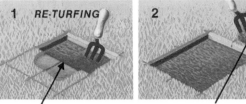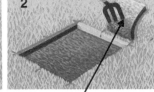

1 RE-TURFING

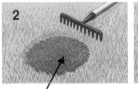

2

3

Bare patches can be caused in a number of different ways:

Compaction and poor drainage are common reasons for the disappearance of grass. They are serious problems because a large area of the lawn may be affected.

Weed removal, oil spill, under-tree drip, bitch urine burn, fertilizer overdosing and the scalping of bumps by the mower generally produce bare patches which are distinct in outline and limited in area. Excessive wear may be limited or widespread, depending on the situation . . . and the number of children.

Wherever possible, try to remedy the cause before carrying out the repair, or the bare patch may quickly return.

Remove dead patch of turf and square up affected area. Then break up the soil surface with a hand fork.

Loosen soil under the new turves with a hand fork. Place them in position.

Firm down the new turves and fill in cracks with sifted soil.

1 RE-SEEDING

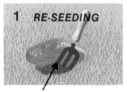

2

3

Prick the surface of the affected area with a hand or garden fork.

Rake thoroughly to remove debris and to form a fine seed bed. Sow seed at 1 oz per sq. yard.

Cover area with a thin layer of sifted soil and press down with a board. Protect from birds with crossed strands of thread.

SUCKERS

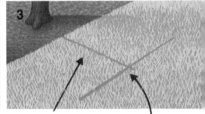

Many shrubs and trees may produce suckers from their roots — examples are lilac, roses and willow. Mowing is made difficult if the shoots are allowed to become established in the lawn — mower blades can be damaged.

Cut turf with spade or edging iron. The cut into the lawn should be along the line of suckers.

Peel back the turves carefully. Chop out the root bearing the suckers.

Firm down the rolled-back turf.

Fill cracks with sifted soil.

RE-EDGING

As shrubs and trees mature they frequently extend beyond the edge of the lawn. This happens all too often when a vigorous conifer is planted in a small island bed.

Mowing becomes difficult, and if the uncut grass is left to grow into the shrubs the effect is unsightly. The bushes can be kept constantly trimmed, but it is often a better idea to move back the lawn by cutting a new edge.

To avoid the problem occurring in future, remember that the small compact plant you buy in a container may grow into a spreading man-sized bush in a few years. Always check on the expected height *and* width at maturity before planting a shrub or tree in close proximity to your lawn.

TREE ROOTS

A tree growing in a lawn sometimes pushes one of its roots above the surface. This is a serious problem — at best mowing becomes difficult, at worst the mower blades are damaged.

If the root is slender it can be chopped out, using the technique described above for suckers. Occasionally the root is too large to deal with in this way, and then the best plan is usually to create a bed around the tree by cutting back the turf. The result is that the root is no longer in the lawn.

Where this is not possible, a workable but less satisfactory alternative is to add soil to form a gently sloping mound covering the root. Firm down this soil (there must be at least a 2 in. layer above the root) and then seed or turf the surface.

New Lawn Troubles

BARE PATCHES

Bare patches in the newly-sown lawn are due to the absence of seed or to faulty germination. The possible causes are:

Poor preparation of the site. Patchiness is often due to the presence of areas of subsoil which have been brought up to the surface by faulty cultivation.

Poor weather conditions. Dry spells on light land and prolonged wet spells on heavy land are frequent causes of patchiness.

Birds

Old seed

Uneven germination. Seed rot kills grass seed before germination. This trouble is worst when the soil is not free-draining, the seed is old and the weather cold and damp. Treating the seed with a fungicidal seed dressing before sowing is a useful preventative.

PATCHES OF YELLOWING OR DEAD SEEDLINGS

If the seedlings have blackened at the base and toppled over, the cause is **damping off disease.** The yellowed plants can be easily pulled out of the soil, and the trouble will rapidly spread unless it is treated at once. Water the affected and surrounding area with Cheshunt Compound at the rate of ½ oz in 1 gallon of water per sq. yard. Damping off is most likely to occur where seed has been sown too thickly and when the weather is humid. The Bents are more susceptible than other lawn grasses.

If the seedlings have not toppled over, then the cause is not an infectious one:

Poor preparation of the site. Subsoil left on the surface by the builder or lawn maker is a common reason. Buried bricks and rubble are also a frequent cause of discoloured patches in the newly-sown lawn.

Poor weather or soil conditions. Both dryness and waterlogging of the surface inch of the seed bed can cause the yellowing and subsequent death of grass seedlings.

YOUNG GRASS THIN AND SPARSE

Sometimes the germination and grass growth appear satisfactory but a complete green carpet is not formed — far too much bare earth is present between the seedlings. There are several possible causes:

Seeding rate too low. Use 1–1½ oz per sq. yard or follow the instructions on the package.

Birds. Not a common reason — birds are more likely to cause scattered bare patches.

Poor preparation of the site. The mistakes usually responsible are insufficient attention paid to the drainage, lack of a crumb structure in the surface inch and the presence of subsoil in the surface layer. You can try feeding, but this will not remove the basic problem.

YOUNG GRASS SLOW-GROWING AND PALE

It is sometimes found that the young grass turns pale green and almost ceases to grow. If this happens in the spring, a stimulant containing nitrogen is required to increase the vitality of the plants. On no account should Lawn Sand or a combined fertilizer/weedkiller be used at this early stage. Use a liquid fertilizer and be careful not to overdose. Use a fine-rose watering can and take care not to disturb the surface. If the grass is only a few months old, apply a liquid fertilizer at the lowest concentration rate listed on the package or bottle, but poor growth at this early stage usually indicates a problem other than food shortage.

CRACKS IN THE TURFED LAWN

Turves occasionally shrink, leaving ugly gaps between them. The cause is invariably the failure to water thoroughly enough and frequently enough in dry weather. The effect is heightened if the turves are not butted closely together at laying time and if sandy soil was not brushed into the cracks after turfing. To repair the cracks, water the lawn and then wait until the turves have expanded back to their original size. At this stage brush top dressing into the cracks— never apply the top dressing first and then water afterwards.

CRACKS IN THE SEEDED LAWN

Cracks may appear in the soil surface of the seeded lawn. This is due to lack of water — a frequent problem in the April-sown lawn on heavy land. Water the whole area, top dress the site of the cracks and then sow a thin sprinkling of grass seed. If a prolonged dry spell occurs after this treatment, remember to water *before* the cracks appear.

HOLLOWS

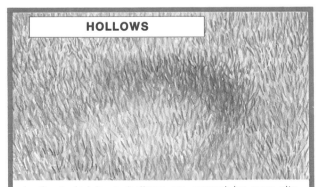

In the turfed lawn, hollows are caused by poor site preparation or carelessness at turfing time. Settlement of an improperly consolidated site can also be the cause of hollows in the seeded lawn, but there are other possibilities here. Birds may have used the seed bed as a dust bath or heavy rain on a sloping site may have created gullies. The answer in all cases is to top dress on a little-and-often basis.

WEEDS

If you have fallowed the site properly (Step 7, page 95), you should not have a serious weed problem in the newly-sown lawn. Of course, some weeds will grow and the appearance of the common flower-bed invaders may appear quite frightening. However, such weeds as groundsel, chickweed, fat hen, couch grass, nettles, bindweed, mayweed and ground elder will die out quite rapidly once mowing starts as they cannot tolerate regular scalping.

It is the weeds illustrated and described on pages 59–77 that you have to worry about, and when these are found you should hand weed. Choose a day when the soil surface is firm, then hold the grass down with one hand and gently pull out the weed with the other. Do this while they are still small.

Occasionally the number of weeds appearing on the new lawn makes hand weeding quite impractical and they may be sufficiently numerous to threaten the existence of the seedling grasses. As noted earlier you only have yourself to blame by being in too much of a hurry. It is vital that before sowing seed the land has been fallowed by hoeing the site regularly or by clearing annual weeds with a chemical treatment. You must not try to solve the problem by the use of a selective weedkiller — 12 months must elapse between sowing seed and the use of one of these products.

STONES

Stones can work their way up to the surface in the newly-sown lawn, and many a mower blade has been damaged by the gardener forgetting to look over the surface before mowing at this early stage in the life of the lawn

Renovating a newly-sown lawn
The thin areas and bare patches should be raked, taking care not to alter the level of the surface. Use the same seed as sown previously, and mix one part of seed with 10 parts of sifted sandy soil. Spread this evenly over the raked area at the rate of ¾ lb per sq. yard. Lightly rake in the seed after sowing.

Mowing Troubles

SCALPING

Scalping is all too familiar — high spots shaved bare by the mower. A cylinder mower is more likely to cause scalping than a rotary model, and the control of this problem calls for several remedial measures. Raise the height of cut if your lawn is bumpy and improve its evenness by top dressing. Never press downwards on the handle when mowing and never use a push-and-pull action as you take the mower across the lawn.

HOVER SCALPING

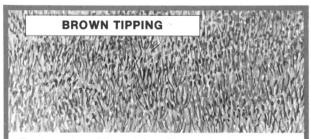

Ordinary scalping is usually the fault of the lawn surface or cutting height and not the way you use the mower, but hover scalping occurs through not following the maker's instructions. If you allow the air cushion to be lost by running the mower over the edge of the lawn then the air cushion is deflated and the blades will shave the grass below. Another cause is re-starting the mower on the flat instead of tilting it to one side as recommended by the manufacturer.

BROWN TIPPING

The browning of the cut tips after mowing is a common problem and there are a number of possible causes. The most likely reason is using a rotary mower with dull blades — the grass is bruised instead of being cut cleanly. Always sharpen rotary blades regularly — it is a simple job to do. With a cylinder mower check the setting and inspect the bottom plate for damage. Another cause of brown tipping is cutting the lawn when the grass is wet.

RIBBING

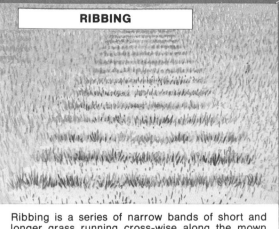

Ribbing is a series of narrow bands of short and longer grass running cross-wise along the mown strip. It is due to the use of a cylinder mower in which the blades are revolving too slowly. Ribbing is much less of a problem now that motor mowers have become popular, but it is still occasionally seen. The answer is to remove the cause of the excessive resistance to the blades — the grass may be too long (cut more frequently), the mowing height may be too low (raise the cutter blades) or the grass may be wet (sweep off raindrops or dew before mowing). Another cause of ribbing is using a hand-driven cylinder mower which has insufficient blades — see page 28.

WASHBOARDING

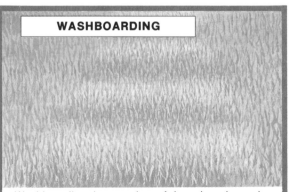

Washboarding is a series of broad and regular corrugations running cross-wise along the mown strip. The effect is wave-like, and the crests are about 6–12 in. apart. It is caused by always mowing in the same direction — this sets up a vibration pattern which eventually produces a ripple effect in the surface soil. Unlike ribbing, this problem has increased with the appearance of the motor mower — with a power-driven machine you should change the direction of cut each time you mow. If washboarding is already present in your lawn, top dress each autumn until a level surface is restored, although the unsightly appearance will often disappear without any treatment once you change the mowing direction.

CHAPTER 5

LAWN CARE PROGRAMMES

RENOVATION PROGRAMME FOR THE NEGLECTED LAWN

It is not uncommon to find yourself the owner of a badly neglected lawn. You may have just moved into a house where the garden has been left unattended for some time, or you may have been unable to look after the lawn because of sickness or prolonged absence from home. Whatever the cause, the neglected lawn is a depressing collection of overgrown grass and weeds.

1 **Carefully examine the grass and weeds** covering the lawn. If moss, pearlwort and various other weeds almost completely dominate the wisps of surviving lawn grasses, then the best plan is to start again, following the rules for the construction of a new lawn laid down in Chapter 7.

In most cases it will be found that despite the presence of tufts of coarse grass and numerous weeds, the desirable lawn grasses still make up the main part of the lawn. Here, remaking the lawn is not necessary and the best plan is to follow a renovation programme as outlined below.

2 **Cut down the tall grass and weeds** to about a couple of inches from the ground. A billhook can be used but only use a scythe if you are skilled in the art. The best plan is to hire a large rotary mower. Rake off the cut vegetation. Spring is the best time to begin this renovation programme.

3 **Re-examine the lawn surface** and, using Chapter 4 as your guide, make a list of the lawn troubles which are obviously present.

4 **Rake and thoroughly brush the surface** so that dead vegetation and rubbish are removed.

5 **Mow with the blades set as high as possible**. Over the next few weeks progressively lower the height of cut until the recommended level is reached (see page 31).

6 **Feed and weed the lawn** in early summer using a combined dressing through a wheeled distributor. Treat patches of moss or algae with a dichlorophen product.

7 **Water in summer and feed if necessary in autumn**. Do not let drought spoil all the good work of stages 1–6 — water thoroughly in prolonged dry weather (see pages 38–39). Use an autumn lawn fertilizer in September if the turf is still thin and pale especially if the turf was not watered in summer.

8 **Shortly afterwards carry out all the necessary lawn repairs** (see pages 82–83). Remember to re-seed or re-turf any bare patches.

9 **A little later spike compacted areas and apply a top dressing**. If the lawn is thin and open at this stage, it is a good idea to mix a little grass seed with the top dressing so that about ½ oz of seed per sq. yard is applied.

10 **Beginning in the following spring, the normal lawn management programme can be followed** (see pages 88–89).

WEEDING AND FEEDING PROGRAMME
FOR THE WELL-MAINTAINED LAWN

There is no such thing as the 'right' programme for every lawn and there is no point in pouring money down the drain by applying treatments that aren't necessary. On the other hand some problems can get rapidly worse if you don't treat them promptly, so the only answer is to keep a careful eye on your lawn and then use the correct product or products for the problems you find there.

The simplest routine is to follow a step-by-step diagnosis in April, June and September. Listed on these two pages are the simple questions you will need to ask during these three inspections.

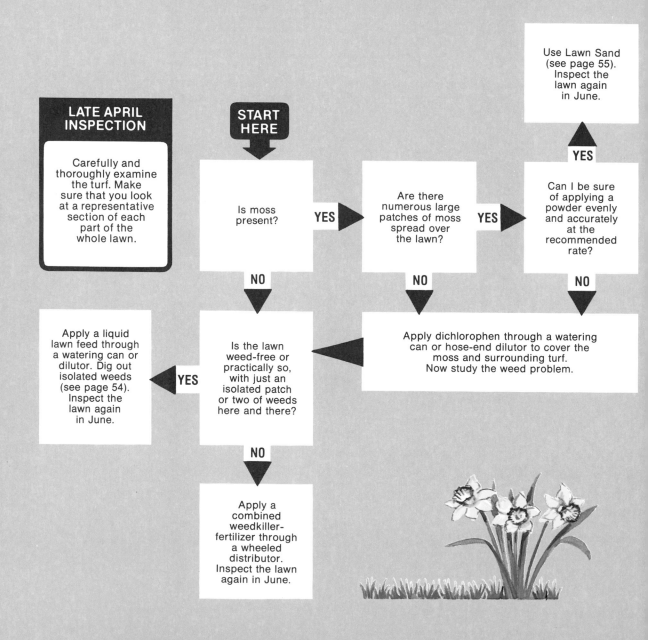

LATE APRIL INSPECTION

Carefully and thoroughly examine the turf. Make sure that you look at a representative section of each part of the whole lawn.

START HERE

Is moss present? **YES** → Are there numerous large patches of moss spread over the lawn? **YES** → Can I be sure of applying a powder evenly and accurately at the recommended rate?

YES → Use Lawn Sand (see page 55). Inspect the lawn again in June.

NO → Apply dichlorophen through a watering can or hose-end dilutor to cover the moss and surrounding turf. Now study the weed problem.

Is the lawn weed-free or practically so, with just an isolated patch or two of weeds here and there?

YES → Apply a liquid lawn feed through a watering can or dilutor. Dig out isolated weeds (see page 54). Inspect the lawn again in June.

NO → Apply a combined weedkiller-fertilizer through a wheeled distributor. Inspect the lawn again in June.

JUNE INSPECTION

Carefully and thoroughly examine the turf. Make sure that you look at a representative section of each part of the whole lawn.

START HERE

Are weeds a serious problem?

NO → **Are a number of isolated weeds or weed patches present?**

NO → **Is the lawn off-colour?**

NO → No chemical treatment is required. Inspect the lawn again in September.

YES ↑ Apply a liquid lawn feed through a watering can or dilutor. Inspect the lawn again in September.

YES ↓ Apply a mixture of liquid fertilizer and weedkiller through a watering can. The addition of fertilizer improves the weed-kill as well as greening-up the turf. Inspect the lawn again in September.

YES ↓ **Is the lawn off-colour?**

NO → Spot-treat the weeds with a ready-to-use weed gun or a liquid weedkiller through a watering can. Inspect the lawn again in September.

YES ↓ Apply a combined weedkiller-fertilizer, unless it was applied in spring. Alternatively water the lawn with a liquid feed and then spot-treat the weeds with a lawn weedkiller through a watering can. Inspect the lawn again in September.

SEPTEMBER INSPECTION

Carefully and thoroughly examine the turf. Make sure that you look at a representative section of each part of the whole lawn.

START HERE

Is moss a problem?

YES ↓ Apply dichlorophen through a watering can or hose-end dilutor.

NO ↓ **Are there numerous worm casts scattered over the surface?**

NO → **Are patches of disease (see page 50) beginning to appear in the lawn?**

NO → **Was a compound fertilizer containing phosphates and potash as well as nitrogen used on the lawn this season?**

YES ↓ Apply Lawn Sand next spring.

YES ↑ Apply carbendazim plus an autumn lawn fertilizer.

YES → **Was the appearance of the lawn disappointing in the second half of the season?**

NO ↑ No chemical treatment is required.

YES ↑

NO ↓ Apply an autumn lawn fertilizer.

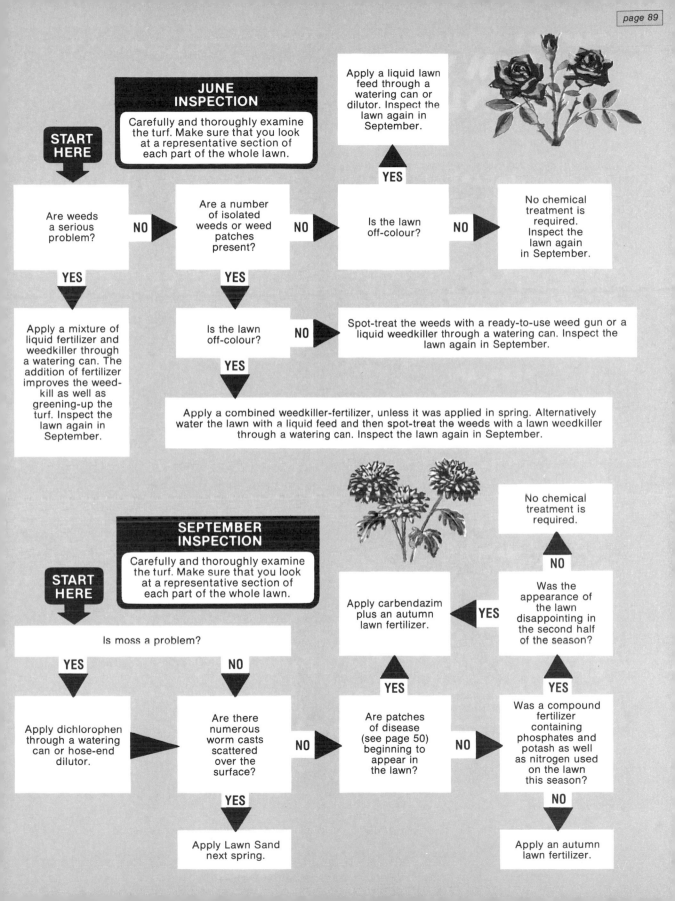

CHAPTER 6
LAWN CALENDAR

JANUARY

There is very little work to do on the established lawn this month, apart from removing fallen leaves. You can do nothing to help the grass in the wet and often bitterly cold weather, but you can harm it by walking on the waterlogged or frozen turf.

This is a good time to have the mower overhauled and to make sure that the other lawn tools are ready for use in the spring. Turfing is possible during a fine spell.

FEBRUARY

In mild districts the lawn care season may begin this month with the appearance of worm casts — scatter them with a besom when they are dry. Do not be tempted to mow your lawn before March arrives.

Finish turfing this month. If you plan to sow seed, begin soil preparation at the end of the month if the weather is suitable.

MARCH

The lawn work programme really starts this month. As soon as the grass has started to grow and the weather and ground conditions are favourable, rake the lawn to remove leaves and surface rubbish. Do not rake too vigorously at this stage or you will damage the grass. If there have been heavy frosts during the winter, it is a good idea to settle the turf by light rolling. A cylinder mower with the cutting head held high is a good method — see page 46.

The first cut should merely remove the top of the grass — close cutting at this stage could result in severe yellowing. Choose a day when the surface is dry — two cuts are sufficient this month.

Mowing isn't the only lawn job in March — look for the early signs of disease, apply a moss killer if necessary and neaten the edges with a half-moon edging iron. Broken edges can be repaired this month — see page 82.

APRIL

Feeding and weeding can begin towards the end of the month, provided that the grass and weeds are actively growing. Follow the guide on page 88 to ensure that you are not carrying out any unnecessary treatments. If Lawn Sand is used, make sure that it is spread evenly and that the dead moss is raked up a fortnight later.

Mow often enough to stop the grass growing away, but do not cut lower than ¾–1¼ in., depending on the type of lawn — see page 31.

Dig out patches of coarse grass — fill the holes with sifted soil and then re-seed or re-turf. Check new turf — refill joints if necessary.

MAY

Continue mowing, increase the frequency as necessary and lower the height of cut closer to the summer level (see page 31). Once a week mowing starts in May.

In most seasons this is the best month for weed killing with either a selective weedkiller or Lawn Sand. Remember the need for dry grass, moist soil and a fine still day when using a weedkiller. If annual meadow grass or clover is present, brush or rake the patches before mowing.

The soil is usually moist in May but a prolonged dry spell can occur. If this happens, water before obvious signs of distress appear and always irrigate copiously — see page 38.

JUNE

Summer mowing should now be under way — twice a week cutting will be necessary when the soil is moist. If there is a long dry spell, raise the height of the cut and do not use the grass box.

This is the time for summer feeding and weeding. If the lawn is off-colour, use a quick-acting nitrogen feed such as sulphate of ammonia or a proprietary liquid one. Spot-treat weeds which have survived earlier treatment. Raking before mowing is important for keeping the runners of clover under control.

Trim the edges regularly and be prepared to water if there is a dry spell. Hot weather this month may have baked the surface soil — it is often a good idea to prick the surface lightly before irrigating (see page 45).

JULY

Mow regularly at the summer height, water if dry weather is prolonged and rake occasionally as recommended for June.

If clover, pearlwort and/or yarrow suddenly appear as problems, use a good selective weedkiller containing 2 or preferably 3 active ingredients. July is a little late for maximum effect, but these weeds should never be ignored.

Holidays can be a problem. If possible, make lawn-cutting arrangements in your absence if you are to be away for a fortnight or more.

AUGUST

The same general treatment as for July. If the grass is overgrown on your return from holiday, do not cut it at the summer height. Tip it at this first cut, then reduce the height of cut for subsequent mowings (see page 31).

August is the last month of the year for weedkilling and for feeding with a nitrogen-rich fertilizer. Seed sowing can begin in late August.

SEPTEMBER

The autumn programme begins this month with the increasing interval between mowings and the raising of the height of cut to the autumn level, which is a quarter of an inch above the summer cutting height (see page 31).

Worms may become active — there are no longer any chemical worm killers so brush away the casts and increase soil acidity next year by applying Lawn Sand in spring. Use an autumn lawn fertilizer now if the lawn is pale and thin. Carry out lawn repairs during showery weather at the middle or end of the month. Bumps, hollows, broken edges and bare patches can be rectified by following the instructions on pages 82–83.

The September routine for all lawns is to scarify first (see page 43), then spike any compacted areas (see page 45) and finally top dress if you can possibly spare the effort and time for this vital operation (see page 35).

If disease patches have already appeared, use the systemic fungicide carbendazim (see page 50). Tackle moles this month — September is truly a busy month on the established lawn!

It is also a busy time for the new lawn — this is the best period for sowing seed but turf laying should be delayed until next month.

OCTOBER

Regular mowing comes to an end during October. For the last cut or two, raise the cutter height and brush off dew or raindrops before cutting. The edges of the lawn should be trimmed for the winter.

Apply an autumn lawn fertilizer, carry out lawn repairs and complete the scarify-spike-top dress routine if these jobs were not tackled last month. Brush up fallen leaves, which would harm the grass and increase the worm problem if left on the surface. Dig out tufts of coarse grass, then re-turf or re-seed the bare patches. If moss is present, use dichlorophen and not Lawn Sand at this time of the year.

On the new lawn, seed sowing should have been completed but the ideal time for turf laying is only just beginning.

NOVEMBER

If the weather is 'open' (neither frosty nor wet) and the surface is firm, mow once with the blades set high. All equipment should now be cleaned and oiled for winter storage. Brush away worm casts and if numerous use Lawn Sand next spring. Keep the lawn clear of fallen leaves and other debris.

November is far too late for seed sowing but it is a good month for laying turf.

DECEMBER

Apart from brushing away leaves, December is the slack end to a busy year. Keep off the lawn when it is wet or frozen — if you must wheel heavy loads over it, put down boards to prevent rutting.

Turfing is possible during a fine spell.

CHAPTER 7

THE NEW LAWN

The grass in your lawn can come from seed or turf. The choice between them may have to be made only once in the life of your garden, so consider the relative merits and drawbacks carefully before making your decision.

Small sprigs of grass for planting a lawn, so popular some years ago, are no longer available. But novel forms of planting material continue to appear — now there are the seeded turves which are unrolled like a carpet.

	SEED	STANDARD TURF	SEEDED TURF
Advantages	**Sowing seed is the cheapest method of lawn production** Effort as well as money is saved — there are no heavy turves to lift and lay. You can also pick your day for lawn making — unlike turf, seed does not quickly deteriorate after purchase so you can wait days or even weeks for suitable weather. You can pick a mixture of grasses which will be suitable for your conditions and the grade of lawn you require. Unlike turf, you will know exactly which grasses you are buying.	**Laying standard turf is the quickest traditional method of lawn production** In a matter of a few weeks a mature-looking lawn is obtained, ready for use and immune to all the seedling troubles such as damping off, birds, cats and annual weeds. A fine seed bed does not have to be produced and turf is laid in late autumn or winter, the quietest period of the gardener's year. The bare ground is given instant colour, and the edges of the new lawn are clearly defined.	**Laying seeded turf is the newest method of lawn production** Like sowing a seed mixture, the 1 sq. yd or 3 sq. yd rolls of seeded turf provide specified varieties of lawn grasses. These rolls are quicker to lay than standard turf, and the weight needed to cover the new lawn is considerably less. It can be cut with an ordinary pair of scissors. Like standard turf, instant colour is provided in the new garden, and there are none of the headaches of seed germination and early establishment.
Disadvantages	The preparation of the seed bed must be thorough — weed removal is very important. The recommended months for sowing are busy times for the gardener, and the young seedlings are at risk from all sorts of problems — bad weather, birds, disease and so on. Until grass has covered the surface, there is always the risk of weed colonisation. A period of 9–12 months must elapse after sowing before the lawn is ready for normal use.	Turf will cost you several times more than grass seed to make a new utility lawn. For a luxury lawn the difference in price is even greater. Much of the turf offered for sale contains a high proportion of coarse grass and numerous weeds — good-quality turf is hard to obtain. Turf has to be laid as soon as possible after delivery, but the recommended time for turf laying is often the worst for getting on the land.	Seeded turf is more expensive than the standard turf used for lawn making, and the luxury grade of seeded turf is much more expensive than a fine-grass seed mixture. A level surface is essential — you cannot easily correct bumps and hollows as you can when laying strips of standard turf. The number of suppliers is strictly limited and there is as yet no long-term garden experience of this new development in lawn making, although it has been used professionally for some years.
Laying or sowing time	**Best: Mid August to mid September** **Next best: April**	**Best: October to February** **Next best: March to April**	**Depends on type of seeded turf — see page 98**
In a nutshell . . .	1–1½ oz seed spread evenly 3 ft 3 ft Lightly rake in seed after sowing	Note bonding of turves Meadow turf Cumberland turf 3 ft 3 ft Brush top dressing into cracks after laying	Note large size of turves 12 ft 12 ft Brush top dressing into cracks after laying
For further details	**See page 96**	**See page 98**	**See page 98**

PREPARING THE SITE

There should be a gap of at least three months between the start of site preparation and the laying of turf or the sowing of seed. This may seem a long time but there are a number of jobs to do and the soil must be given time to settle before the final smooth surface is created. Work should start in early summer for autumn sowing or turfing.

STEP 1

SPRING
OR
EARLY
SUMMER

Get down to bare earth

If you have moved into a new house, clear away the bricks, rubble, rubbish and piles of subsoil left by the builder.

The site of a new lawn is usually an overgrown patchwork of weeds and grass. First, dig out tree stumps and roots — left in the soil they could lead to a toadstool problem later on. Next, dig out perennial weeds and treat the area with paraquat/diquat. Alternatively spray all weeds with glyphosate.

Think carefully before leaving any trees within the proposed lawn area. Trees and lawns really do not go together — see page 8.

STEP 2

EARLY
SUMMER

Grade the site (Omit this step if levelling is not required)

The purpose of grading is to change the contours of the site so that the approximate final level is obtained. Note that the lawn does not have to be perfectly horizontal — a slight slope will help drainage. However it should be level, without any bumps and hollows — gentle undulations are acceptable in a large lawn but are out of place in a small plot.

HOW TO OBTAIN A LEVEL SURFACE

1 in. 1 in. — Several wooden pegs

Painted line 4 in. from top

Straight-edge board 7 ft long

Spirit level

(1) Choose a day when the soil is reasonably dry. Set the pegs to the desired level

6ft

6ft

(2) Then add or remove soil from between the pegs until the soil surface is level with the painted lines on each peg

GRADING A SITE WITH MINOR BUMPS AND HOLLOWS

Do not shave off the tops of the bumps to fill the hollows unless the topsoil is deep. It is better to bring in topsoil from elsewhere in the garden or to buy a load for this purpose.

GRADING A SITE WITH MAJOR BUMPS AND HOLLOWS

Remove the topsoil and stack it at a convenient point. Make all the alterations with the subsoil. When the desired level has been obtained, replace the topsoil. On no account should subsoil be brought to the surface. If the topsoil layer is less than 6 inches thick, buy a load or two from a local supplier.

GRADING A SLOPING SITE

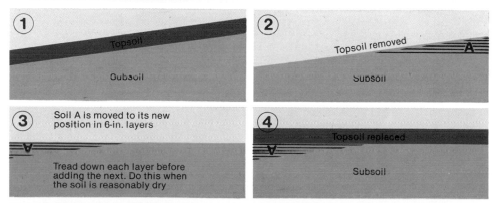

(1) Topsoil / Subsoil

(2) Topsoil removed / A / Subsoil

(3) Soil A is moved to its new position in 6-in. layers. Tread down each layer before adding the next. Do this when the soil is reasonably dry

(4) Topsoil replaced / Subsoil

PREPARING THE SITE continued

<table>
<tr><td>

</td><td>

Drain the site (Omit this step if the site does not waterlog)

Good drainage is essential for a first rate lawn, and it is fortunate that thorough digging and the addition of soil improvers (see Stage 4 below) are all that is required for most soils. You may be unfortunate enough to have a site which is clayey and where water remains on the surface after heavy rain. Some form of drainage is essential here, or the lawn will rapidly deteriorate.

If levelling is undertaken, put in the drainage system when grading (Step 2). If levelling is not necessary, put in the drainage system when digging (Step 4). Simple systems are described below — tile drainage is elaborate and costly.

</td></tr>
</table>

SIMPLE DRAINAGE SYSTEM FOR A SLOPING SITE

Construct one or more soakaways at the lowest part of the site

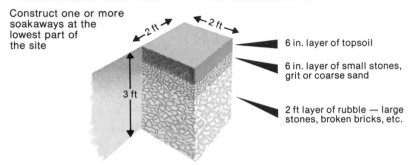

- 6 in. layer of topsoil
- 6 in. layer of small stones, grit or coarse sand
- 2 ft layer of rubble — large stones, broken bricks, etc.

SIMPLE DRAINAGE SYSTEM FOR A LEVELLED SITE

Before replacing the topsoil after grading, spread a layer of rubble on the subsoil and press it well down. Add a layer of grit or coarse sand then replace the topsoil.

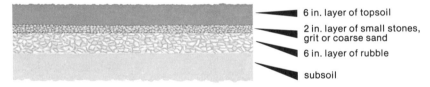

- 6 in. layer of topsoil
- 2 in. layer of small stones, grit or coarse sand
- 6 in. layer of rubble
- subsoil

TILE DRAINAGE SYSTEM — EFFECTIVE, BUT EXPENSIVE

Very few gardens warrant the costly and elaborate system of laying drainpipes in gravel-lined tunnels, but it is undoubtedly the best method of draining a site which has a subsoil of impervious clay.

<table>
<tr><td>

</td><td>

Dig the site

Digging should be done with a fork or spade to a depth of about 9 inches, or less if the topsoil is shallow. Do not bring up the subsoil — if there is less than 6 inches of topsoil, you should buy a load or two to make up the deficit. The right time to dig is controlled by the weather — the soil must be reasonably dry. Depending on the soil type, the addition of sand or peat may be necessary at this stage.

If you are not used to digging, the cultivation of an average-sized plot can be exhausting and even dangerous if you are not fit. Consider hiring a mechanical cultivator — it may not be as effective as a fork or spade but it will certainly be less tiring. Whichever method you use, large stones and the roots of perennial weeds should be removed as the work proceeds.

</td></tr>
</table>

HEAVY SOIL
Work in at least 28 lb of lime-free sand per sq. yard when digging. If subsoil is clay, fork the bottom of the trench to the full depth of the prongs.

LIGHT SOIL
Work in about 7 lb of peat per sq. yard when digging.

STEP 5

SUMMER

Break down the clods

If the clods left after digging are not properly broken down, then settlement is bound to occur later and your lawn will be uneven. The problem of bumps and hollows in established turf is difficult to cure, but it is easy to prevent.

All you have to do at this stage is to trample the roughly dug earth with your feet. As you proceed break up hard clods with either a heavy metal rake or the back of a garden fork — remove debris, weeds and large stones at this stage.

If the site is large you can use a rotary cultivator set to work at a shallow depth. Whichever method you choose for breaking down the clods, you must pick a day when the soil is reasonably dry.

For autumn sowing or turfing this step will have to take place shortly after digging, but if the soil is heavy and you plan to sow in April, then delay breaking down the clods until spring.

STEP 6

ABOUT
A WEEK
LATER

Firm the site

The next step is to consolidate the soil and produce a reasonable tilth in the top inch or two. Once again your feet are the best tool to use — walk with short overlapping steps with all your weight on your heels. Choose a day when the soil is fairly dry — on no account should the top few inches be saturated with water.

The soft spots will be revealed by deep footprints. Rake the surface level and remove stones and debris. Repeat the treading and raking process until the site is firm enough not to show deep heel-marks, yet soft enough to have a crumbly structure in the top inch or two.

A garden roller is sometimes recommended for firming the soil but this can be an unsatisfactory method. Air pockets are often left, and when they eventually settle an uneven surface is produced.

STEP 7

FROM
FIRMING
UNTIL
STEP 8

Fallow the site

The purpose of fallowing is to get rid of the dormant weed seeds which could germinate and cause a problem in the new lawn. This step is therefore necessary where seed is to be sown but is much less important prior to turfing.

The traditional method is to hoe and then rake at about monthly intervals throughout the summer, but this makes site preparation a lengthy job. The simplest plan is to hoe the site regularly if weeds appear during the period between firming and the time you plan to sow seed. Alternatively, let the weeds develop after firming and apply paraquat/diquat just before Step 8.

STEP 8

JUST
BEFORE
SOWING
OR
TURFING

Get the site ready for sowing or turfing

You have now reached the final stage. Use a long straight plank to check whether the soil is level — rake gently to remove bumps and fill in hollows.

If you plan to sow seed or if the site to be turfed is distinctly bumpy, you will need a more accurate method of levelling. Attach a rope to a ladder, as illustrated, and drag this home-made screed over the surface after the top inch or two has been loosened by raking.

The site is now ready for seeding or turfing. When seed is to be sown, there should be very few lumps on the surface which are larger than a grain of wheat.

SOWING SEED

To reach the stage of the final seed bed takes a lot of hard work and patience. In contrast, seed sowing is a simple and straightforward task, but carelessness at this stage can undo all your hard work.

The most important pitfall is buying a poor seed mixture which will inevitably lead to a disappointing result. You can do this by purchasing a 'bargain' mixture, full of broad-leaved Perennial Ryegrass, or you can buy a perfectly good seed mixture ... which just happens to be quite wrong for your particular needs and situation. Avoid the pitfall of buying the wrong seed by reading the section below *before* you go shopping.

Seed Mixtures

There is no such thing as the perfect seed mixture for every situation — **the right one for you will depend on the type of lawn you have in mind (luxury or utility grade) and the type of site you have in the garden (shady, sunny, clayey or sandy)**.

Don't be swayed by pretty pictures, pretty names or glowing sales messages. Read the package carefully to make sure that it meets your needs. If you have decided on a luxury lawn (see page 11), then you will want a mixture of Fescues and Bents. You will not find much variation here — most of the mixtures available are similar to the formula given on the right.

Utility Grade Mixtures, on the other hand, vary enormously. Basically they consist of a mixture of fine-leaved and coarser grasses drawn from the species listed on pages 12–13 and 16–17. Remember that the more expensive mixtures can usually be relied upon to contain better varieties than the cheaper blends.

It has long been the practice to divide Utility Grade Mixtures into cheap blends containing Perennial Ryegrass and distinctly superior blends which contain no Perennial Ryegrass. The recent introduction of the dwarf and fine-leaved varieties of Perennial Ryegrass, such as Lorina, Gator, Hermes and Talgo, makes this division less meaningful these days. A simple rule to follow if you want a top quality utility lawn is to avoid a mixture containing Perennial Ryegrass unless the package makes it quite clear that a low-growing, fine-leaved variety of this grass has been used.

If your site is either particularly clayey or very sandy, check that the mixture is suitable for such a situation or buy a tailor-made blend. There are mixtures for shady sites, but cutting higher and less frequently than normal are more important here than buying a special mixture.

Typical Blends

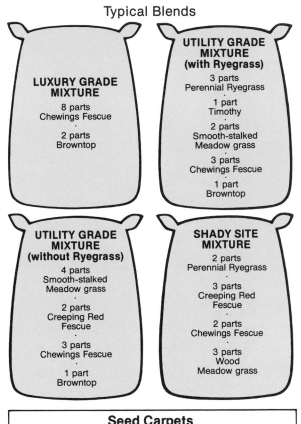

LUXURY GRADE MIXTURE

8 parts
Chewings Fescue
.
2 parts
Browntop

UTILITY GRADE MIXTURE (with Ryegrass)

3 parts
Perennial Ryegrass
.
1 part
Timothy
.
2 parts
Smooth-stalked
Meadow grass
.
3 parts
Chewings Fescue
.
1 part
Browntop

UTILITY GRADE MIXTURE (without Ryegrass)

4 parts
Smooth-stalked
Meadow grass
.
2 parts
Creeping Red
Fescue
.
3 parts
Chewings Fescue
.
1 part
Browntop

SHADY SITE MIXTURE

2 parts
Perennial Ryegrass
.
3 parts
Creeping Red
Fescue
.
2 parts
Chewings Fescue
.
3 parts
Wood
Meadow grass

Seed Carpets

Grass seed embedded in a fibrous or plastic mat has been available for many years, but these grass-seed carpets have never become popular. They are easy to lay, but they have to be anchored securely after laying and they are of course more expensive than ordinary seed.

① Feed the soil

Unless the plot has been recently fed, apply 2 oz of Growmore per sq. yard about a week before the final preparation of the seed bed (Stage 8, page 95). Lightly rake into the surface.

② Choose the right day

The best time of the year is early or mid-September when the soil is still warm and the chance of a water-shortage problem is declining. April sowing is often successful but watering will be necessary if the summer is dry, and watering is a tricky operation on the newly-sown lawn.

Choosing the right day is also important. The top of the soil should be dry with moist soil just below the surface. Delay sowing if mud is sticking to your boots. The weather should be fine and calm.

③ Sow the seed

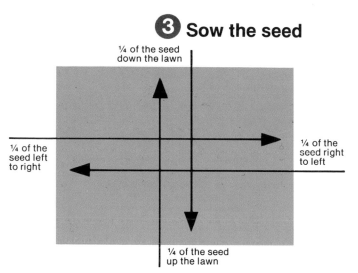

¼ of the seed down the lawn

¼ of the seed left to right

¼ of the seed right to left

¼ of the seed up the lawn

Buy sufficient seed to allow an application rate of 1–1½ oz per sq. yard. Lower rates may mean that the lawn remains thin and sparse for an unnecessarily long time — higher rates increase the risk of damping off (see page 84).

Gently rake the surface soil in straight lines so that very shallow furrows are produced. Shake the box or bag of seed thoroughly and weigh out the amount required to cover the site — remember you will have to sow about 3 in. beyond the edge of the final size of the lawn you have planned. Next, divide the seed into four equal parts and then sow each part as evenly as possible — see the illustration. By sowing in quarters the errors of distribution and the chance of missed patches are reduced. Instead of broadcasting the seed by hand, a distributor can be used. In this case apply half the seed across and the other half up and down the site.

④ Protect the sown seed

The two immediate enemies are water shortage and birds. To help combat the first problem, lightly rake the whole area with a spring-tine rake to partly cover the seeds. Do not try to bury them or germination will be patchy. Rolling the seed bed after sowing used to be recommended. Don't do it.

The second problem can be a serious one. The use of bird repellent by the seedsman will have reduced the risk of birds using the seed as a source of food, but it will not prevent birds from using the seed bed as a dust bath. The answer is to criss-cross strands of black thread 3 or 4 inches above the ground. Stand on a plank and not on the seed bed when you do this job.

⑤ Trim and care for the seedlings

Time of sowing	Time taken for shoots to appear
Autumn	1–2 weeks
Spring	2–3 weeks

The seedlings will appear 7–21 days after sowing. If rain has not fallen for several days at the time of germination you may have to water the plot. Take care to do this very gently — use a fine-rosed watering can or a lawn sprinkler which produces a fine spray. A coarse spray may wash the seedlings out of the ground.

When the grass is 2 or 3 inches high, remove any stones and then gently sweep away worm casts and leaves on a day when the surface is dry. Follow this with a light rolling using the back roller of a cylinder mower with the cutter head held high. This treatment firms the soil lifted by the germinating grass and encourages the seedlings to produce new shoots.

After a few days the shoots will once again be erect and the time has come for the first cut. Only the top ½ inch of the grass should be removed and the mower blades *must* be sharp. Use a sidewheel mower, a rotary mower or a roller mower with the front roller removed. On an autumn-sown site no further cutting will be required until the spring — on a spring-sown site regular mowing will be necessary and the blades should be gradually lowered.

⑥ Take care of the new lawn

Although the young grass may look healthy and vigorous, the new lawn should be tended carefully and not subjected to any heavy traffic for 12 months after sowing. Water carefully when necessary, and keep a careful watch for disease right from the beginning. Weeds can be an additional problem — see pages 84–85 for the diagnosis of and cure for new lawn troubles.

LAYING TURF

The disadvantages of turf compared with seed as a method of producing a new lawn are both obvious and important. Good turves are expensive and hard to find, and you can never be sure of getting just the grasses you want unless you invest in seeded turf. So the golden rule is to make sure you get value for money by examining a sample before you buy and then examining the turves at laying time.

Turves can be obtained in a number of sizes, ranging from 1 sq. foot to 3 sq. yards, with 1 ft x 3 ft as the most popular size. Turfing is heavy work, but it has an attraction which for many outweighs all of the disadvantages — the bare soil is transformed into a 'finished lawn' in the span of a few hours.

Buying turf

Cheapest of all and by far the most popular type is **Meadow turf**. Unfortunately the farmer's idea of good grass is almost completely opposed to the needs of the gardener, and there may be hardly any lawn grasses present. Good quality Meadow turf can produce a hard-wearing utility lawn, but poor quality Meadow turf merely provides a sea of weed grasses. Obtain a sample before you buy it — if this is not possible, tell the supplier that you expect lawn turf and not rough grassland.

The turf covering the South Downs is made up almost entirely of fine-leaved grasses, and **Downland turf** is much better than the ordinary Meadow variety. Best of all is **Parkland turf**, stripped from a site close to your home.

The legend of **Cumberland turf** (sea-washed turf) as the best of all types still persists. It is obtained from salt marshes and is composed of Creeping Red Fescue and Creeping Bent. Unfortunately it is difficult to maintain once it is away from its coastal habitat and nearly always deteriorates quite rapidly in the hands of the amateur gardener.

Seeded Turf

Seeded turf first appeared on the amateur market in 1980, but it has been used for a number of years in landscape gardening and the construction of sports grounds. Unlike standard turf, which is cut from meadows, salt marshes etc., this new form is obtained by sowing lawn grasses on a suitable substrate. The resulting turf is weed-free, composed entirely of desirable lawn grasses and is much lighter in weight than standard turf.

	Mature grass type	Seedling grass type
Age of grass	12–18 months	8–10 weeks
Base	Soil (½ in. thick)	Growing medium on a plastic mesh
Size of roll	16 in. x 81 in.	30 in. x 132 in.

THE SIGNS OF GOOD TURF

No pests or diseases

Good uniform colour — desirable lawn grasses clearly present. No bare patches

Recently mown. Long growth can disguise thatch, small-leaved weeds, etc.

Virtually no weeds

Good soil, neither clayey nor distinctly sandy. No stones present

Good underground growth — plenty of white roots present

Uniform thickness 1–1½ in.

Final test: Lift it up by holding one end with both hands. Shake it gently up and down. It should not tear nor fall to pieces

❶ Order the turf

Find a reputable supplier and buy the best quality you can afford — the cheapest grade is bound to produce a poor quality lawn. Order about 5 per cent more than the calculated area to allow for wastage. There may not be a choice in turf sizes, but you should remember that small turves are much easier to lay than large ones. Plan exactly where the turf is to be stacked — do this *before* the lorry arrives!

❷ Feed the soil

Unless the plot has been recently fed, apply 2 oz of Growmore per sq. yard about a week before the final preparation of the plot (Stage 8, page 95). Lightly rake into the surface.

❸ Get the plot ready

Mark out the area to be turfed, using a garden line for the straight edges. Curves are more difficult to mark — scratch out a shallow drill with a stick and fill this boundary line with sand.

❹ Get the turf ready

Standard turves (1 ft x 3 ft) will be rolled up when delivered to you. Laying should take place as soon as possible after delivery — turf can deteriorate quite quickly.

If the turf is to be laid within 3 days of delivery

Store in a stack 3–4 turves high

If the turf is to be laid more than 3 days after delivery

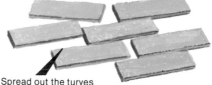

Spread out the turves in a shady spot. Water if necessary

❺ Choose the right day

The best time of the year is October or November, but turfing can continue right up to February provided that the soil is neither frozen nor waterlogged. You can turf in March or April, but this will mean regular watering when the weather is dry — failure to do so will mean shrinkage of the turves and death of the roots.

Choosing the right day is also important. Laying turf in the rain is a filthy job, so pick a fine day when the soil is reasonably dry.

❻ Lay the first row of turves

① START with a single row along the side of the site closest to the stack of turves

② TAMP DOWN each row of turves with a tamper made from thick boards and a pole. Gently press them down, don't beat them down!

③ CHECK THE LEVEL with a board and spirit level after tamping down. If there are bumps and hollows *never* beat the turf down with the back of a spade. You should lift the turf and add or remove soil as necessary

Inspect each piece of turf before placing it in position — pull out any rosette weeds. If it is full of weeds and coarse grasses, reject the piece and place it on the compost heap. If many of the turves are unusable and you bought 'good quality' material, complain strongly to your supplier

❼ Lay the second row of turves

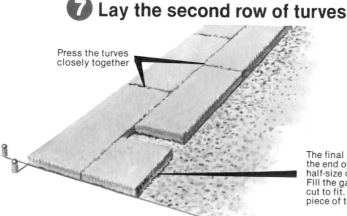

Press the turves closely together

The final piece to be laid at the end of a row should be a half-size or full-size turf. Fill the gap behind with a piece cut to fit. Never use a small piece of turf at the edge

LAYING TURF continued

⑧ Finish laying the turves

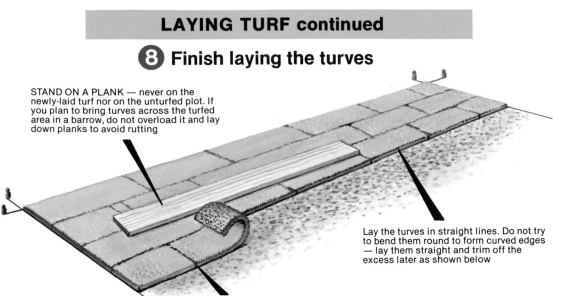

STAND ON A PLANK — never on the newly-laid turf nor on the unturfed plot. If you plan to bring turves across the turfed area in a barrow, do not overload it and lay down planks to avoid rutting

Lay the turves in straight lines. Do not try to bend them round to form curved edges — lay them straight and trim off the excess later as shown below

Note that the edges of the turves in adjacent lines are staggered like bricks in a wall

⑨ Fill the cracks

Make up the top dressing recommended for heavy soil — see page 35. Spread this sandy soil along the cracks and work it well into the turves with a broom or the back of a rake. This will help the turves to knit together. This step is essential — an additional job, which is not essential, is a light rolling of the new turf about 7 days after laying.

⑩ Trim the edges

Trim the edges with a half-moon edging iron. Stand on a board — use it as your guide if you are cutting a straight edge. For curves use a hose-pipe as your guide, as shown in the illustration

⑪ Take care of the new lawn

When the grass begins to grow in spring you will have to start the new-lawn establishment programme. First of all, cut the lawn with the blades set high, so only the tips of the grass leaves are removed. As the season progresses the blades should be gradually lowered until the recommended height of cut (see page 31) is reached.

In late April or during May apply a quick-acting fertilizer. Top dressing at this stage will help to smooth out any minor bumps and hollows, and a weedkiller can be used on autumn-laid turf. Remember that the new lawn is more susceptible than established turf to damage by drought, so water thoroughly during prolonged dry spells.

CHAPTER 8
A LAWN MISCELLANY

TURNING CLIPPINGS INTO COMPOST

Lawn clippings are notoriously difficult to turn into compost, as the standard method calls for mixing them with other waste matter in which there is an abundance of fibrous material. The usual advice is to make a heap in which no more than one-third is made up of clippings from the lawn.

Unfortunately the volume of lawn clippings during late spring and summer often greatly exceeds the supply of other waste greenstuff to make a suitable compost mixture. In this case the Recycler method should be used. This is suitable for clippings alone or for mixed garden waste, but you must remember that the procedure is quite different from the standard rules for compost making. In the Recycler method soil is an essential ingredient, the heap must never be turned and you should keep it covered to keep out the rain.

The secret is to keep in as much heat as possible, so make the heap as large as possible. Plastic bins are much better than ordinary plastic bags and boards or bricks around the sides of an ordinary open heap can make all the difference.

There are five simple steps:

1 Make a layer of clippings about 9 in. deep.

2 Spread a layer of finely-chopped or shredded carbohydrate-rich material over the surface. You can use oatmeal, coarse bran, shredded newspaper or sawdust. As a guide 2 small handfuls should cover about 10 sq. ft.

3 Cover with a thin layer of soil. A 1 in. layer will provide an abundance of bacteria and will also absorb the water and gases which can stop the compost-making process.

4 Continue in this way until all the clippings are used.

5 Cover the top to keep out rain.

Next time you mow simply repeat the process on top of the previous pile. A heap that was made in spring or summer can be used in late autumn or the following spring. If the grass has been recently treated with a selective weedkiller, leave at least 6 months between placing the clippings on the heap and using the compost.

GRASS PATHS

Lawn books all deal at length with the preparation and maintenance of sizeable areas of turf, but many ignore the grass path. This is unfortunate because in a great number of gardens there is a strip of grass between beds, borders and/or rockery, and it is these grass paths which are especially difficult to maintain.

The problem is the concentrated amount of traffic which it has to bear. For this reason spiking, top dressing, regular feeding etc are especially important. Wherever possible avoid grass paths which are less than 3 ft wide.

GETTING ADVICE

You can take a sick child to the doctor or a sick puppy to the vet., but there is no garden doctor you can visit when something has gone wrong with the lawn. Despite this, there are many sources of sound advice.

First of all, study the relevant page or pages of this book when there is a problem. A visit to your favourite garden shop or garden centre seems the obvious next step, and no doubt you will find there a number of free advisory leaflets and plenty of lawn products. But do be careful when seeking advice — by all means be guided by a trained and competent assistant, but your lawn may suffer if you rely on the word of a keen but totally inexperienced employee!

A letter or a telephone call to a national supplier can be a great help — the leading seed, machinery, chemical and fertilizer companies all have advisory services and will happily provide an answer to your specific problem. However, you cannot expect them to prepare garden designs or analyse soils for you. If you have to send a specimen of the turf, call first and find out the correct method of packing.

Join your local Horticultural Society. You will be able to attend lectures and also meet fellow lawn owners who may have had similar problems. The knowledge of experienced members is especially helpful if you are new to gardening. Also consider joining the Royal Horticultural Society — members are entitled to seek advice on all aspects of gardening.

Magazines can be useful — all the leading ones have advisory services and will provide written replies to lawn care enquiries. Some journals require a stamped-addressed envelope — check the query page before sending off your problem.

THE HISTORY OF THE LAWN

B.M. — Before the Mower

Historians have written about the lawns which appeared in Persian, Greek and Roman gardens before the birth of Christ, but the evidence for their existence is extremely scanty. The first detailed picture we have of the early lawn is drawn from continental manuscripts produced between 1300 and 1500.

The Advantages of Country Living describes how they were made. The site was cleared of all weeds and roots and the ground was sterilized with boiling water. Turves cut from good grassland were then tamped down on the levelled earth — not too far removed from the instructions on pages 98-100!

The Romance of the Rose reveals what the Mediaeval lawn looked like. From this famous book and other illustrated sources we know that it was not composed of grass alone — it was a "flowery mead" studded with pinks, periwinkles, primroses and many other low-growing plants.

It is often forgotten that all the information about the lawns of this period is derived from continental sources — there are no detailed British records. We do know that the troubled Middle Ages were times for fighting and not gardening in this country, and so it seems certain that our early lawns were pale imitations of the elegant expanses in Italy and France.

It was inside the castle walls that the English lawn began. There was an area of grass on which the knights and their ladies could walk and sit — well away from the smells and vermin of indoor living. There were turf-topped seats and also rectangular 'greens' on which games such as bowls and pell-mell were played — it is interesting that from the very beginning there seems to have been a division into ornamental and sports turf. Outside the castle walls, the monastery garden within the cloisters was another ancestor of the lawn of today.

In Tudor and Elizabethan times the garden became a place to be adorned and admired. Around the vast mansions and palaces of the day spread long grassy pathways between the beds, large 'plats' were created for bowls and other games, and grass-covered mounts looked down on the splendour of England's new wealth. The lawns were not always composed of grass; the chamomile lawn was obviously popular — books gave cultural instructions, Falstaff noted that "the more it is trodden the faster it grows" and Drake is supposed to have bowled on a chamomile lawn whilst the Spanish Armada waited. The garden lawn was born, but it was no better than its counterparts across the Channel.

In about 1610 the Jacobean age of gardening began, and so did a feature which was henceforth to arouse the envy of gardeners everywhere — the closely-cut British lawn. No one man could have created this concept, but Francis Bacon is usually regarded as its High Priest — "The green hath two pleasures, the one because nothing is more pleasant to the eye than green grass finely shorn, the other because it will give you a fair alley in the midst". Guides to lawn-making appeared in many books, but the one which is usually quoted is the Gervase Markham translation of *La Maison Rustique*. In an otherwise sound set of instructions, Markham noted that the turves should be placed grass *downwards* on the earth. Many have commented on this 'unusual' technique, but nobody seems to have made the obvious suggestion that it could have been a mistranslation or a misprint!

By the end of the Jacobean period the admiration for the English lawn was established — d'Argenville, one of France's greatest horticultural authors, wrote in 1709 "The grass plots are so exquisite in beauty, that in France we can scarce ever hope to come up to it."

Gardening fashions change, and at the beginning of the 18th century William Kent "leaped the fence, and saw that all nature was a garden". The age of the landscape garden, le jardin anglais and Capability Brown had begun. Now grass, trees and water filled the whole estate and the regular scything and rolling of vast acreages took place all over Britain.

The Industrial Revolution, the onset of the Victorian Age and the mushrooming of countless small villa gardens changed the face of gardening in the early 19th century. Gardens were now filled with beds, terraces and statues. The lawn decreased in size — the work involved in scything meant that it would have had no place around the homes of ordinary people, if it had not been for the invention patented by an obscure foreman working in a textile factory in Stroud. The year was 1830 and the man's name was Edwin Budding …

A.M. — After the Mower

The introduction of the mower resulted in the rapid decline in the use of the scythe as a lawn tool. There was a steady stream of new ideas, patents and improvements after 1830. The American 'Archimedean' mower appeared in Britain in the 1860s, bearing a single spiral blade and the revolutionary idea that cuttings should be left on the lawn as they would keep it "fresh and green even in the hottest summer, and this without any untidy appearance whatever." Obviously, bold claims by lawn mower manufacturers began a long time ago!

One of the most important developments was the introduction of alternative sources of power to tired arms and an aching back. The first horse-drawn mower appeared in 1842 and the first steam-driven machine was made in 1893. Petrol-driven mowers have a long history — they were cutting the lawns of the wealthy in the first years of the 20th century. The most important breakthroughs for the ordinary gardener were the introduction of the lightweight electric mower in the 1960s and the launch of the hover mower by Flymo in the late 1960s.

Many lawn aids apart from the mowing machine were introduced in Victorian times. There were wheeled lawn edgers, wheeled lawn sweepers and knapsack sprayers, but above all in importance was the introduction of rubber hosing by the Gutta Percha Company.

Budding's invention was the cylinder mower, adapted from the device which trimmed the pile on cloth in the factory where he worked. In 1832 Ransomes went into production, and suddenly keeping grass neatly shorn became an unskilled and relatively speedy job. There was a small model at 7 guineas "for a gentleman who wishes to use it himself" and a larger 10 guineas version which was "preferable for workmen."

There were various methods of keeping grass under control before Budding's invention. In the Mediaeval lawn there had been much trampling and beating to suppress growth, and in the landscape garden of the 18th century a variety of animals such as sheep and cows grazed the grass around the grand houses of the day. But it was scything which quickly established itself as the standard technique. The early guides recommended scything twice a year, but the British lawns of the 17th century were cut twice a month.

This relatively frequent cutting aroused the envy of overseas visitors, but it did involve a great deal of hard work. The turf was rolled a few days before scything, and after cutting it was the job of a team of women to gather up and dispose of the clippings. We shall never know what the average lawn looked like in those pre-mower days. One author wrote that a good workman with a scythe "will leave it very nearly as smooth and even as the piece of green cloth which covers the table on which I am writing." The truth, however, may well have been closer to the description of the results of scything in Budding's patent — "circular sears, inequalities and bare patches...... which continue visible for several days."

The character of the turf depends on the species of grasses which are present, and even the early text books warned against the use of ordinary farm grasses. "The best turves for this purpose are had in the most hungry common..." wrote John Rea in 1665, so it is surprising that research into lawn grasses began so late. The first trials started in 1885 — this early American work showed that Bents and Fescues were the best grasses for the luxury lawn. It was the golf craze which prompted these investigations — the first experimental turf garden was established in 1890 and quite quickly additional trial sites were created throughout the United States.

Research got off to an ever slower start in Britain. It was not until 1924 that the Green Committee of the Royal & Ancient Golf Club proposed that research into turf culture should be undertaken, and in 1929 a research station was founded at Bingley. In 1951 the original group, known as the Board of Greenkeeping Research, was reorganised as the Sports Turf Research Institute.

Of course, much research has been done and continues to be done by seed, chemical and machinery producers. In recent times there have been many advances in feeding, weeding, disease control, lawn making, etc., and there is no sign that this steady stream of innovation is coming to an end. This book carries details of equipment and techniques which were unknown when the first edition was written; no doubt some future edition will describe machines and chemicals which are unknown today.

THE U.S. LAWN

"Your lawns are so beautiful" has been said so often by horticulturally-minded tourists from the U.S. after driving through Britain and seeing a never-ending ribbon of front lawns. There are two reasons for this supposed superiority compared with the turf in many areas of America. Because of our favourable climate we are able to grow fine- or fairly fine-leaved grasses all over the country and there is no winter browning — a state of affairs which applies to only part of the U.S. Secondly we cut the grass shorter than they do in America and this gives the characteristic short-pile carpet look. The U.S. lawn owner has all sorts of problems the British gardener does not have to face. Insect damage is much more common and there are weeds which are not found in Europe. In many areas prolonged drought occurs every year and not just occasionally, so sophisticated watering systems are necessary. It is therefore not surprising that American homeowners have to spend more on their lawns than their British counterparts. Despite their efforts at home many U.S. tourists will continue to envy the British lawn, but throughout the U.S. there are countless superb lawns which put the average U.K. expanse of turf to shame.

GRASS TYPES

There are two basic climatic zones which govern which types of grass can be grown. The cool season zone has warm summers and cold winters, and here you will find the grasses described on pages 12–13 and 16–17 or their close relatives. Bents, Fescues, Meadow grasses (Bluegrass in the U.S.) and Ryegrasses dominate the scene, but the varieties and their relative importance differ — the most popular species is Kentucky Bluegrass (Poa pratensis). The warm season zone lawn is quite different — here the species must be able to grow actively in hot summers and lay dormant during the cool winter months. Examples include Zoysia, St Augustine Grass, Bermuda Grass and Centipede Grass.

Zoysia

MAKING A NEW LAWN

As in Britain the usual starting point is seed or turves (sod in the U.S.) although in the warm season zone both plugs (small pieces of sod) and sprigs (pieces of creeping stem) are popular. A mixture of different grasses is generally used for seed sowing in the cool season zone but once again the southern states are different — here it is quite usual to buy grass seed which is a single variety when making a lawn.

MOWING

Except for luxury lawns made up of fine grasses such as Creeping Bent the recommended cutting height is approximately 2 in., which is about double the height recommended for British lawns. The recommended frequency of cutting is, however, the same — when the grass has grown by about 50 per cent of the recommended height of cut then it is time to mow. This may mean every couple of days or every few weeks depending on the grass type and situation, but for most people on both sides of the Atlantic mowing is a weekend job during the active growing season.

WATERING

The various techniques outlined on page 39 are employed in the U.S. but there is an important addition — in lawns in the warm season zone the use of pop-up sprinklers is widespread whereas in Britain they are an expensive and unusual novelty.

CHAPTER 9

OTHER WAYS TO COVER THE GROUND

The earlier editions of this book dealt almost exclusively with the grass lawn — the other sorts of ground-covering materials were covered briefly in just a couple of pages in the Miscellaneous section at the end.

In this edition there is this whole chapter devoted to all of the alternative types of ground cover which are available. The book is still called The Lawn Expert and it is of course the grass lawn which takes pride of place with 100 pages describing every facet of the turf which adorns our gardens. But some of the alternatives have become increasingly important during the past few years and so other ways of covering the ground are dealt with here in some detail.

There are three main reasons why the role of ground covers other than lawn grass has become more prominent. First of all there is the recent promotion of the no-lawn concept for small front gardens. Not too long ago the idea of tearing up the lawn in front of a terraced or small semi-detached house and replacing it with paving or gravel together with a collection of pots or beds would have been frowned on, but not now. These days it is fashionable for some garden designers to recommend this approach, and the reasoning behind it has some merit. It is sometimes difficult to transport a mower to the front of the house and there is often dense shade which means a constant battle against moss. However, it is your house and there is no reason whatsoever for getting rid of a mini-lawn if it is reasonably healthy and you prefer grass to an expanse of stone or brick. The rows of front garden lawns along suburban and inner city streets are part of our national scenery and it would be sad indeed if they disappeared in the name of 'good' garden design.

The second reason for the increase in interest in alternatives to grass lawns is the rather romantic view that our gardens should have a more natural look. As a result much is written these days about the wildflower meadow. The photographs taken in spring look most attractive on the printed page, but in reality this form of ground cover is difficult to create and even more difficult to maintain. As noted later in this chapter the wildflower meadow can be an interesting feature tucked away in a large garden, but it can give the garden a decidedly untidy look if it is a prominent display in a small garden. The ordinary meadow filled with rough grassland and naturalised spring bulbs is usually more satisfactory. Non-desirable weeds can be kept down with a weedkiller and there are fewer restrictions on the time of mowing.

The third and final reason why this section on ground-covering methods has been extended in this edition is the growing appreciation of the value of ground cover plants between trees and shrubs. Some are evergreen so that there is living colour between the leafless shoots of deciduous shrubs in winter. Others may bear flowers or foliage which is non-green so that the visual appeal of the area is enhanced. If well chosen and properly maintained the living carpet provided by ground cover plants is certainly a great improvement on bare soil, but the most important virtue is its ability to suppress weeds.

In the following pages you will find descriptions and pictures of six different ways of covering the ground without using turf. In the main your best plan is to consider them as ways of adding to the appearance of the garden alongside but not replacing the turf. If the situation is right then there is nothing which can match the beauty of a well-tended lawn.

THE MEADOW

The meadow is an area of land which is completely or primarily covered with semi-rough grass. Like a lawn it will tolerate foot traffic but unlike a lawn it is cut at protracted intervals of a month or more.

The most appealing advantage is immediately obvious — the chore of weekly mowing is removed. There is another advantage — in the right setting the meadow has a more natural and sometimes a more attractive appearance than a closely-shorn lawn. The meadow, however, is not for everyone. It has no place in the small front lawn, except perhaps under a shady tree. In a larger lawn the furthermost part can be allowed to become a meadow in which spring bulbs can be naturalised and allowed to die down after flowering before cutting begins. It is in the very large garden where the meadow really comes into its own — close to the house the grass is treated as lawn and beyond that there is the meadow or parkland.

The difference between a lawn and a meadow is fairly clear cut, but the dividing line between a wildflower meadow and a meadow is not quite as clear. It would indeed be a strange meadow which did not have a scattering of wildflower blooms in early summer, but there is still a difference.

In the meadow these flowers arise from weeds which are in the soil and are not on plants which have been specially sown or planted. Due to the long gaps between cutting the wildflowers are often accompanied by undesirable plants such as thistles, docks and nettles which would have been controlled if mowing was frequent and regular. This weed flora can give the area a distinctly untidy look — in the meadow a lawn weedkiller can be used to keep them under control, but this must not be done in a wildflower meadow.

Creating a meadow with fast-growing grasses on rich soil can be a disaster — the sea of long grass and ugly weeds can look like a completely neglected piece of wasteland. A really successful meadow calls for using the right seed on the right soil which has been properly prepared. Do not regard a meadow as an easy option when starting from scratch.

PREPARING THE GROUND

It may seem odd that the requirements for a really satisfactory meadow are fussier than for a lawn, and it may cost you more to prepare the site before sowing or turfing. The first basic principle is that you don't want the grass to grow too quickly and that means the soil should have low fertility for good results — sandy free-draining ground is best of all. The next basic principle is that killing weeds at this stage is more important than it is when preparing the ground for making a lawn. The reason is that in the lawn the perennial weeds in the ground are slowly killed by regular mowing but this does not happen in a meadow. Vigorous weeds will romp away, especially if the grass is cut only twice a year, so before you begin to cultivate the site prior to seeding or turfing it is necessary to use glyphosate to kill the weeds growing on the surface. Spot treat or spray overall depending on the amount of weed cover. The ground can now be prepared by following the rules in Chapter 7 with just a couple of exceptions — do not fertilize the site and there is less need to aim for a truly level surface.

BUYING SEED OR TURF

In most cases the meadow will already be in existence or you will have decided to allow part of your lawn to have a more natural look by cutting it less often and thereby turning it into a meadow. In these situations you will have no control over the grass varieties which are present and you will have to control the growth of over-vigorous grasses by mowing. The position is different if you are starting from scratch as you can exercise control over the type of grasses which will make up your meadow: Here your aim should be to use a seed mixture of low-growing grasses — note that low-growing does not necessarily mean slow-growing. If you are starting from turf try to obtain material made up of compact grass varieties. The things to avoid are seed mixtures containing old type Perennial Ryegrass rather than one of the modern dwarf varieties or turf cut from an agricultural meadow which will contain high productivity grasses.

LOW MAINTENANCE MIXTURE	
Perennial Ryegrass Lorina	6 parts
Creeping Red Fescue	3 parts
Browntop	1 part

MOWING & MAINTENANCE

The rules for when to cut are fairly straight-forward for the established lawn (see page 31) but not for the established meadow. With the meadow the timing and frequency of mowing depend on whether the area contains natura-lised bulbs and your own personal taste concerning how long the grass should be. The rules for the new meadow are more clear cut. With a sown meadow lightly trim the seedlings when they are about 3 in. high and cut every couple of weeks to about this height. When starting from turf aim to maintain the same height as for the newly sown meadow and mow at fortnightly intervals. In both cases you will have to remove unsightly perennial weeds by grubbing out with a small fork or trowel as weedkillers cannot be used for 12 months after sowing seed or for 6 months after laying turf. The frequency of cutting the meadow once it is established is less well defined. If you have naturalised spring bulbs in the meadow then you will have to wait 6 weeks after the last of the flowers have faded before you can start mowing. If bulbs are not present the first cut should be made in late June. The time for the next mowing after this first one depends on the effect you are trying to create and the time you are trying to save. Just one more cut in September is all that is required if you want a natural look and/or you have very little time to give to the meadow. Some people prefer a neater appearance — the routine here is to cut the grass at about monthly intervals to keep it approximately 4 in. high. Make the last cut in October. Mowing a meadow is not a job for a cylinder mower — use a rotary model or a strimmer. If a weedkiller is to be used you should wait until the leaves of spring bulbs have completely died down.

△

Contour mowing is a way of making a meadow more decorative or a way of allowing easier passage. Strips are cut through it following the lawn rules so that grass pathways are created — sometimes geometric shapes are also mown regularly at lawn height to give a sculptured effect.

NATURALISING BULBS

'Naturalising' means growing bulbs in a manner and situation that make them look like wildflowers in open grassland or in grass under trees. To achieve this effect is not quite as easy as it sounds. First of all only a limited number of bulbous plants are small enough not to look out of place, vigorous enough to compete with grass, hardy enough to stand up to our winters and prolific enough to spread rapidly over a period of years. Next, the grass must be managed in such a way as not to harm the bulbs and any trees above must be open enough to enable the bulbous plants to develop and flower properly.

There is one basic consideration you must take into account if you want to use bulbs in this way. It is essential to wait at least 6 weeks after the last flowers have faded before cutting the grass. The reason is that the leaves must be left to produce the food for the developing bulbs below ground — the bulbs which will provide next year's show. These remarks concern the spring-flowering bulbs which are the most popular type of planting material — with autumn-flowering bulbs you must stop cutting the grass at the beginning of September to let the shoots develop. The first step is to choose the bulbs — a single species or a mixture of types can be used. It is up to you but the purists consider that just one type is the better choice. The next job is to cut the grass and then planting can begin. A bulb planter can be used, but the turf-lifting method shown on the right is generally much more satisfactory. Whichever method is used it is vital to avoid a geometric planting pattern — the classic technique is to drop a handful of bulbs on the ground and plant them where they fall. As a general rule the tips of small bulbs should be about 2 in. below the surface and larger ones at 4 in. deep. A favourite place is under trees in the meadow — some can tolerate shade but most grow and flower before the leaves on the trees are fully open.

Use a spade to cut the ground to the required depth and fold back the turves as shown. Replace turves after planting and firm down by walking over the area.

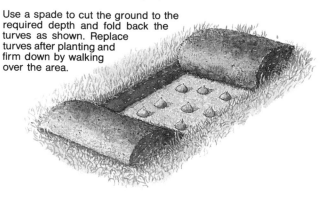

NATURALISING IN OPEN GRASSLAND:
Camassia • Colchicum • Erythronium • Fritillaria • Galanthus • Leucojum • Muscari • Narcissus • Ornithogalum • Scilla

NATURALISING UNDER TREES:
Allium • Anemone • Arisaema • Arum • Brimeura • Eranthis • Erythronium • Fritillaria • Galanthus • Ipheion • Leucojum • Lilium • Muscari • Narcissus • Ornithogalum • Scilla • Trillium • Tulipa

Not all of these bulbs are wildflowers — see pages 110–113 and The Bulb Expert for more information

THE WILDFLOWER MEADOW

The 'flowery mead' was a basic feature of the mediaeval garden, but its popularity declined as fashion dictated that there should be a clear separation between beds, borders and lawns. In recent years there has been a renewal of interest in the flowery mead or flowering meadow. The idea of having an area of fine-leaved and low-growing grasses liberally sprinkled with a wide variety of wildflowers has caught the public imagination for several reasons. Primarily it is linked with our greater interest in the environment. Poppies, Cornflowers, Ox-eye Daisies and so on are less plentiful than they used to be because of increased urbanisation and modern farming practices, and the wildflower meadow in the garden seems to be a way of redressing the balance in a small way. A second attractive feature is the idea that mowing is an occasional rather than a regular task and the third reason for the increased interest in the wildflower meadow is their regular appearance these days on television, at major horticultural shows and in gardening magazines.

A couple of words of warning. Unless you are really into the Green Movement it is unwise to turn your whole garden into a wildflower meadow — for much of the year it will have an uncared-for appearance. Create this feature at the back of the carefully-tended area, and even here it will only be attractive and labour-saving if the soil is right, the seed-mixture is suitable for the site, the soil is free from vigorous perennial weeds and you have the right machinery to cut it when mowing is due.

Approach the creation of a wildflower meadow with the acceptance that it may not be an easy option and that at times it may have the ragged look of any natural or semi-natural feature. Then you can get down to creating an area which can make use of land which is too poor to grow anything else and which will be filled with the flowers of the field for you, your visitors and wildlife to enjoy. It is best to start from scratch, but as noted later you can transform an area of existing grassland provided the soil is not rich and the grass varieties are fine leaved and relatively slow-growing.

A–Z OF MEADOW WILDFLOWERS & BULBS

NAME	HEIGHT	FLOWERING PERIOD	NOTES
AUTUMN CROCUS (Crocus speciosus)	4–6 in.	September–October	Violet flowers. Common in wildflower meadows but not a native bulb
BIRD'S FOOT TREFOIL (Lotus corniculatus)	6–15 in.	June–September	Red-tinged, pea-like flowers on trailing stems. Prefers sandy soil
BLUEBELL (Hyacinthoides non-scripta)	8–12 in.	April–May	Drooping blue bells above strap-like leaves. Prefers damp soil
BUGLOSS (Anchusa arvensis)	8–20 in.	June–September	Bright blue flowers on top of bristly stems. Prefers chalky soil
CHICORY (Cichorium intybus)	12–40 in.	July–October	Blue flowers borne in small clusters all along the branched stems
CLUSTERED BELLFLOWER (Campanula glomerata)	6–12 in.	May–September	Stalkless white or mauve flowers in tight clusters. Prefers chalky soil
COMMON DOG VIOLET (Viola riviniana)	1–8 in.	April–June	Flowers are mauve and scentless — for fragrant blooms choose Sweet Violet
COMMON POPPY (Papaver rhoeas)	8–24 in.	June–August	Scarlet flowers on thin stems — once a very common sight in meadows
COMMON ST JOHN'S WORT (Hypericum perforatum)	10–30 in.	June–September	Yellow starry flowers borne in loose clusters. Prefers sandy soil
COMMON STORK'S-BILL (Erodium cicutarium)	12–20 in.	May–September	Small star-shaped pink flowers above ferny foliage. Prefers sandy soil
COMMON TOADFLAX (Linaria vulgaris)	10–30 in.	July–October	Antirrhinum-like yellow flower heads above grey-green leaves
CORNCOCKLE (Agrostemma githago)	12–36 in.	June–August	Reddish-purple flowers on long stalks — no longer common in cornfields
CORNFLOWER (Centaurea cyanus)	6–12 in.	June–August	An annual with bright blue flowers — no longer common in cornfields
CORN MARIGOLD (Chrysanthemum segetum)	6–18 in.	June–August	Related to Ox-eye Daisy, but shorter and flowers are all-yellow
COWSLIP (Primula veris)	6–12 in.	April–May	Drooping yellow flowers less open than Primrose blooms. Prefers chalky soil
CUCKOO FLOWER (Cardamine pratensis)	6–24 in.	April–June	Small lilac 4-petalled flowers on top of stems. Prefers damp soil
DAFFODIL (Narcissus pseudonarcissus)	8–20 in.	April	This is the lemon yellow Wild Daffodil — for showier blooms choose a named one
DROPWORT (Filipendula vulgaris)	12–30 in.	June–September	Similar to Meadowsweet but grows in drier soil and has fewer flowers
DYER'S GREENWEED (Genista tinctoria)	10–24 in.	July–September	A small shrub with spikes of yellow flowers on upright stems
FIELD GENTIAN (Gentianella campestris)	4–10 in.	July–October	Purple tubular flowers on top of upright stems. Prefers chalky soil
FOXGLOVE (Digitalis purpurea)	24–48 in.	June–August	Tubular flowers on tall spikes — spotted inside. Good in shade but poisonous
GRAPE HYACINTH (Muscari armeniacum)	8–10 in.	March–April	Familiar blue-flowered spikes. Common in wildflower meadows but not a native
HAREBELL (Campanula rotundifolia)	6–15 in.	July–September	Pendant blue bells on slender upright stalks. Prefers chalky soil
HORSESHOE VETCH (Hippocrepis comosa)	4–12 in.	June–August	A sprawling plant with golden flowers on upright stems. Prefers chalky soil
KNAPWEED (Centaurea species)	12–30 in.	June–September	Both Black and Greater Knapweed have purplish-red thistle-like flowers
LADY'S BEDSTRAW (Galium verum)	6–30 in.	July–August	The tiny, 4-petalled flowers are yellow. Stems bear whorls of narrow leaves
LESSER CELANDINE (Ranunculus ficaria)	3–8 in.	March–May	Yellow buttercups on long stalks above heart-shaped leaves
LUCERNE (Medicago sativa)	12–30 in.	June–July	Pale purple pea-like flowers on small conical spikes
MARJORAM (Origanum vulgare)	12–24 in.	July–September	Tight heads of tiny mauve flowers above the stems and aromatic leaves
MARSH MARIGOLD (Caltha palustris)	12–24 in.	March–May	Large buttercup-like flowers above heart-shaped leaves. Needs damp soil

Autumn Crocus

Bird's Foot Trefoil

Common Dog Violet

Common Poppy

Corncockle

Cornflower

Corn Marigold

Lesser Celandine

Marjoram

NAME	HEIGHT	FLOWERING PERIOD	NOTES
MEADOW BUTTERCUP (Ranunculus acris)	6–36 in.	June–July	Yellow buttercups on upright stems — common in pastures. Prefers heavy soil
MEADOW CRANE'S-BILL (Geranium pratense)	12–30 in.	May–September	Pale blue or violet flowers above deeply-divided foliage. Prefers chalky soil
MEADOW SAFFRON (Colchicum autumnale)	6–10 in.	September–October	Pink or mauve flowers on leafless stalks — rare in the wild
MEADOW SAXIFRAGE (Saxifraga granulata)	4–20 in.	April–June	Small white flowers on upright stalks above lobed kidney-shaped leaves
MEADOWSWEET (Filipendula ulmaria)	24–40 in.	June–September	Many heads of creamy-white tiny flowers. Needs damp soil
MUSK MALLOW (Malva moschata)	12–30 in.	July–August	Large pink hollyhock-like flowers above deeply-divided leaves
OX-EYE DAISY (Leucanthemum vulgare)	10–40 in.	June–August	Unbranched stems bear yellow and white daisies — a familiar sight in meadows
PRIMROSE (Primula vulgaris)	3–6 in.	February–May	Rosettes of yellow flowers within wrinkled leaves. Prefers acid soil
QUAKING GRASS (Briza media)	8–16 in.	June–September	Decorative grass with triangular flower heads which flutter in the breeze
RAGGED-ROBIN (Lychnis flos-cuculi)	12–24 in.	May–June	The narrow petals give the flowers a ragged appearance. Prefers damp soil
RESTHARROW (Ononis repens)	10–20 in.	June–September	Pink pea-like flowers on creeping stems. Prefers lime-rich sandy soil
ROCK ROSE (Helianthemum nummularium)	3–12 in.	June–July	Yellow papery flowers on the tips of creeping stems. Prefers chalky soil
SAINFOIN (Onobrychis viciifolia)	12–24 in.	June–August	Spikes of pea-like flowers — pink with purple veins. Prefers chalky soil
SALAD BURNET (Sanguisorba minor)	10–20 in.	June–September	Round heads of pink flowers above cucumber-flavoured leaves
SCABIOUS (Knautia or Succisa species)	30–36 in.	June–October	Both Field and Devil's Bit Scabious have lilac or mauve 'pincushion' flowers
SELF-HEAL (Prunella vulgaris)	3–12 in.	June–September	Oval heads of purple flowers. A common lawn weed — prefers short grass
SNAKE'S HEAD FRITILLARY (Fritillaria meleagris)	10–15 in.	April–May	Pendant bells with a checkerboard pattern on top of upright stems
SNOWDROP (Galanthus nivalis)	6–10 in.	January–March	Much-loved herald of spring — drooping white blooms and strap-like leaves
SOFT RUSH (Juncus effusus)	12–48 in.	June–August	Cylindrical stems bear brown flower-heads on one side. Needs damp soil
SPRING SQUILL (Scilla verna)	4–12 in.	April–June	Similar to Star of Bethlehem but flowers are blue or mauve
STAR OF BETHLEHEM (Ornithogalum umbellatum)	4–12 in.	April–June	Spikes of starry flowers which close at night and in dull weather
SUMMER SNOWFLAKE (Leucojeum aestivum)	12–18 in.	April–May	Looks like a Snowdrop but it flowers later and is much larger
VIPER'S BUGLOSS (Echium vulgare)	12–30 in.	June–September	Pink buds open into blue flowers on tall spikes. Prefers sandy soil
WHITE CAMPION (Silene alba)	12–30 in.	May–September	Creamy-white night-opening flowers on upright branching stems
WILD CARROT (Daucus carota)	12–30 in.	June–August	Flat heads of white flowers with a central red one. Large fruit heads
WINTER ACONITE (Eranthis hyemalis)	3–5 in.	January–March	Glossy yellow flowers each with a frilly green collar. Leaves appear later
WOOD ANEMONE (Anemone nemorosa)	4–12 in.	April	White flowers tinged with purple. Prefers woodland but will grow in grassland
YARROW (Achillea millefolium)	6–12 in.	June–September	Flat heads of tiny white flowers above ferny foliage. Prefers dry soil
YELLOW IRIS (Iris pseudoacorus)	24–48 in.	May–July	A good plant for wet grassland — yellow flowers above sword-like leaves
YELLOW RATTLE (Rhinanthus minor)	6–18 in.	May–August	Spikes of yellow hooded flowers on upright stems. Seeds rattle inside fruit

Meadow Buttercup

Meadow Saffron

Ox-eye Daisy

Primrose

Quaking Grass

Self-heal

Snake's Head Fritillary

Star of Bethlehem

Winter Aconite

PREPARING THE GROUND

Read the section on page 107 dealing with preparing the ground for the creation of a meadow. The same general rules apply when making a flowering meadow, but low fertility and weed eradication are even more important. The recommended routine is to spray the area with glyphosate when the weeds are actively growing. If time permits a second application about a month after the first is advisable if the plot is very weedy. One month after the final glyphosate application the top few inches of soil should be stripped off if the land is fertile and if the size of the planned meadow is not too large.

SOWING THE SEED

The first step is to buy a good quality mixture of fine grasses and a variety of meadow wildflowers. You can buy a 'natural' mixture obtained from agricultural meadows, but this may contain weed-type wildflowers which are undesirable. It is better to use a mixture which is made by mixing individual types of seed. Here you have a choice — ready-made mixes under various names (Flower Lawn, Flower Meadow Mixture etc.) are available or you can blend your own from packets bought from a garden centre or specialist supplier. With either route the grass element should consist entirely or predominantly of Bents and Fescues, and the wildflower element should contain numerous varieties which will grow in your situation. As the tables on pages 110 and 112 indicate some wildflowers have quite fussy requirements, so make up or buy a mixture which will be suitable. Some annuals as well as the more usual perennials may be present and the wildflower seed content of branded mixtures is in the 5–20 per cent range.

Autumn is the best time for seed sowing — sow in May if that is not possible. Follow the instructions on the package or use ¼ oz per sq. yard with a home-made mix. Adding fine sand to the mixture will help to ensure even distribution and be careful not to bury the seed when raking it into the surface.

CONVERTING A MEADOW

In most cases the gardener does not start from scratch — it is more usual to try to convert an area of rough grassland in the garden into a wildflower meadow. If the area is small and your aim is to give the patch of semi-wild turf a more natural look, then naturalise some bulbs (see page 108) and plant some suitable wildflowers as described below. After this you can carry on as before with the proviso that you shouldn't cut the grass until the flowers have faded and their foliage has died down. If on the other hand the area is large and you wish to take wildflower gardening seriously then a more careful approach is needed. Omit any feeding and remove all clippings from the area for at least a year before you start and then carry out the conversion in October if you can or in April if you have to wait. Unfortunately sprinkling a wildflower seed mixture over the area is not the way to do it — you will have to start with robust seedlings in small pots or divisions obtained from larger plants. Cut the grass to about 2 in. before you start in order to make the job easier,

and put in approximately one plant per sq. ft — avoid a regular pattern at all costs. The plants you require can be bought ready for planting or raised at home from seed sown in late summer.

MOWING & MAINTENANCE

The mowing plan for a successful lawn may be time-consuming and tedious, but as set out on page 31 it is quite straightforward. This is not so for the wildflower meadow. Here you will need to adjust the frequency of cutting to the vigour of the grass, the wildflower and bulb species present and the growing conditions. There are no hard and fast rules for the established wildflower meadow, but the plan for the newly-established one is more clear-cut.

In the first year the goal is to prevent the grass from swamping the wildflowers and to make sure that the perennials put their strength into leaf and not flower production. The grass should therefore be cut in March, May, July and September at a height of 2–3 in.— do not expect flowers in this first season although some annuals may bloom. Always use a grass box to remove the clippings and get rid of docks, thistles and nettles by grubbing out or spot-treating with glyphosate.

A popular maintenance plan for the established wildflower meadow is to make the first cut when the spring flowers have all faded and set seed. This is generally in late June or early July, and a second and final cut of the season is made in September or October. There are, however, several variations of this basic plan. If growth is vigorous in summer an August cut may be necessary and if you have autumn-flowering plants then the final cut should be delayed until late October or November. When cutting you should aim at a height of 3–4 in. and this can pose problems. If your mower cannot be set to this height you will have to either scythe or use a strimmer. Never apply a fertilizer or an overall weedkiller treatment and always remove the clippings. Ideally you should leave the clippings on the surface for a few days before removing them so that the seeds can fall into the meadow, but this is not really essential.

THE SYNTHETIC LAWN

Synthetic playing surfaces have been used to replace natural turf in numerous areas of the sports world, and it seems that their use will increase over the years. For many gardeners, however, the idea of using plastic lawn at home is an obscenity.

Others, including the author, consider that it can have a role to play in the garden — provided that it is never used where natural grass could be cultivated and maintained. In many gardens there is an area or two which has to support foot traffic but cannot be laid down to grass. Typical examples are balconies, terraces, poolsides and conservatories. The usual answer is to pave the site with stone or concrete tiles, but synthetic turf offers an attractive and lightweight alternative. Like stone it can be hosed down or brushed but unlike stone it is resilient and provides a reasonably natural-looking base for pot plants, as the photograph above clearly shows.

The modern synthetic lawn is made of polypropylene and is available in rolls which are usually 6 ft or 12 ft wide. The grass-like tufts are treated to prevent weathering and fading, and there are no problems in laying or maintenance. But there is one piece of vital advice — always obtain samples from a number of suppliers before purchasing. Some types are surprisingly life-like — others look nothing like grass. Synthetic turf is expensive, costing as much or even more than your living-room carpet, but the cheap sorts can be distinctly disappointing.

Once you have made your choice and received your roll of lawn carpet it will be necessary to prepare the site. It will have to be clean, smooth, firm and dry. Some manufacturers say that their turf can be spread out like a rug, but for satisfactory results you should stick it down with an adhesive — always use the one recommended in the instruction leaflet. The plastic turf can be cut to fit quite easily with a pair of scissors or a sharp knife.

All of this seems a far cry from the naturalness and needs of the grass lawn, but the way to regard synthetic turf is as a substitute for paving stones and gravel, and not as a substitute for natural turf.

THE NON-GRASS LAWN

We use the word 'lawn' as shorthand for a grass lawn — an area of closely-knit grasses which is regularly mown and which is able to withstand some foot traffic. Grass, however, is not the only lawn-making plant. If you like the idea of being different and if you have a well-drained site, then you can create a non-grass lawn. Such lawns may be novel but they are certainly not new. The Chamomile lawn was popular in Elizabethan times, as noted on page 102, and for many years the extensive Chamomile lawns at Buckingham Palace have been admired by the chosen few at the Royal Garden Parties.

Articles on Thyme and Chamomile lawns tend to oversell the idea. There are, of course, advantages compared with the common-or-garden lawn — they are colourful if allowed to flower and sweet-smelling when walked upon. But there *are* serious drawbacks — the plants, though low-growing, do not give a smooth-shaved look and in winter the leaves may turn brown. It is difficult to maintain an even, closely-knit turf but the worst drawback of all is the lack of any chemical to control the weeds without damaging the lawn.

Perhaps the best plan is to create a non-grass lawn on a small plot away from the main lawn. It will need to be bounded by paths, walls, etc. as regular edging is not really practical. It is vital that the ground is weed- and grass-free before you start, so fallowing (see page 53) or an overall treatment with glyphosate is necessary before seeding or planting.

Little or no mowing will be required (use a rotary mower with the blades set 2 in. high) but weeding will be a tiresome task — hand pulling is the only technique available. Apart from Thyme and Chamomile many other plants have been successfully used, and it is not surprising that they are nearly all well-known weeds or their close relatives — Yarrow, Pearlwort, Speedwell, Clover and Moss. In the non-grass lawn the roles are reversed — fine-leaved grasses become common and highly undesirable weeds! So try a non-grass lawn if the idea appeals to you, but remember that grass is the most manageable and reliable planting material for the general-purpose lawn, and it is the *only* planting material for areas which will be subjected to heavy wear.

NON-GRASS LAWN PLANTS

CHAMOMILE

Chamomile (Anthemis nobilis) is a low-growing creeping plant with ferny leaves and white daisy-like flowers. It will stand up to being walked on and the foliage emits a pleasant smell when crushed. Its attraction as a lawn maker is obvious, and Chamomile lawns were grown in this country before the fashion for the closely-mown fine grass lawn began. Despite the age-old history of the Chamomile lawn it has never become popular, and the simple reason is that in nearly all cases the difficulties outweigh the charms.

The starting point is soil which is free-draining, acidic and weed-free. Don't even bother to try to make a Chamomile lawn if your soil waterlogs in winter or is known to be chalky. The less expensive plant material is seed of flowering Chamomile — sow seed in March and plant out in May, setting the seedlings about 6 in. apart. Once established the plants will need occasional clipping or mowing with the blades set high to prevent flowering. A more satisfactory but more expensive approach is to buy young plants of the non-flowering variety Treneague. Use the same planting distance as for seed-raised plants, but clipping or mowing will not be necessary.

Water the plants during dry spells and hand weed as necessary. The appearance of a Chamomile lawn during its first season is often excellent, but unfortunately it usually deteriorates during wet winters and hot summers. Patchiness is almost inevitable as time goes by, and a large Chamomile lawn is almost bound to be disappointing. Aim instead to have a small area which can be tended regularly, and the use of a Chamomile/fine grass seed mix reduces the likelihood of having lots of brown patches. An earth-topped seat on which Chamomile is grown makes an excellent mini-lawn, and patchiness is not a problem if you use this plant as a ground cover around shrubs rather than as a lawn maker.

THYME

It is easier to produce a lawn with Thyme than with Chamomile. It will grow in alkaline and neutral soils as well as acid ones and it is more resistant to dry conditions. It is therefore not surprising that Thyme lawns are more popular than Chamomile ones, but even here some replanting will be necessary every few years. The species to use is Creeping Thyme (Thymus serpyllum) and you will find varieties with white, pink, red or lilac flowers. The starting point is home-grown or nursery-raised seedlings planted out in spring — set out these young plants at 6 in. intervals and keep the area regularly watered until the lawn is established. The usual maintenance routine is to allow the plants to bloom and then trim once the blooms have faded.

PEARLWORT, YARROW, MOSS

These three common lawn weeds are occasionally listed as source material for a non-grass lawn, but they should only be used in special circumstances. It would be plainly foolish to pick one of these instead of grass for a reasonably good site — the only time you should even consider using one of these weeds is when a heavy infestation is already present and grass has been a dismal failure despite all your efforts. The routine is to clear the site of the weeds and grass growing there with glyphosate and then plant small clumps of the weed in question in autumn. In the following season hand weeding of other weeds and grass will be necessary — generally a more difficult task than mowing a grass lawn. Moss and Pearlwort will only flourish in a damp site and browning in winter is a drawback. Yarrow will stay green throughout the year but growth is untidy and the flower stalks are tall.

HARD LANDSCAPING

No one would argue with the use of hard landscaping material such as bricks, gravel or reconstituted stone slabs instead of grass for covering a path, especially if it has to carry heavy traffic. Not everybody, however, would agree with the use of such materials to cover an area of land which could support a lawn.

In most situations a lawn has a charm which cannot be matched by hard landscaping. In summer it is a smooth and soft area for sitting on, playing on or just admiring — in winter it is a living green carpet when so much of the garden is either brown or dead. There is the chore of mowing from spring to autumn, of course, but that is a small price to pay for the benefits of this age-old and basic feature of the British garden.

There is one situation where one should seriously consider replacing a lawn with a hard-landscaped area. This is the small plot in front of a terrace or town house — an area of turf here has to face one or perhaps two serious problems. First there is the shade cast by the house and perhaps by surrounding trees — this lack of light means that there will be a constant battle against moss and sparse grass growth. Secondly there is the difficulty of having to transport the mower to the lawn if there is no garage in which it can be stored. Hard landscaping over the area is the solution recommended by many designers, but for most gardeners in this situation the difficulties of looking after the grass are still worthwhile, and you can find countless tiny grassy gems despite the drawbacks.

If you do decide to follow the hard landscaping route then you should consider the problems before you start. A stone path or gravel walkway may look attractive but do try to picture the *whole* area covered in that way. Next, make sure that the colour and material you choose are in keeping with the house. Finally, remember that hard landscaping can be hard work — don't even think of doing it yourself if the effort is going to be more than you are used to. Even if you are fit and strong you must know what you are doing — read a manual such as The Garden DIY Expert or enlist an experienced friend before you begin. If you can afford it, call in a professional landscaper if the hard work does not appeal to you.

MATERIALS

BRICKS & BLOCKS		No heavy lifting is necessary. Bricks are an excellent choice where an old-world look is required. Don't use ordinary bricks — ask for paving ones. As an alternative you can use brick-like blocks (paviors) made of clay or concrete
STONE & SLABS		Natural stone gives an air of luxury, but slate, sandstone, yorkstone etc. are very expensive. Slabs made of concrete or reconstituted stone are a much more popular and inexpensive alternative these days
MACADAM		This mixture of stone chippings with tar or bitumen has several names — asphalt, black top, 'Tarmac' etc. This is not a job for an amateur — choose your contractor with care. A popular material for drives but too dull for most people as a lawn alternative
CRAZY PAVING		Laying flagstones or paving slabs can be heavy work and you generally have to keep to straight lines — with crazy paving the pieces are smaller and the informal effect means that you don't have to aim for a perfect fit
CONCRETE		Concrete is too austere for large areas, but it remains a popular material for both paths and drives. It is durable, fairly inexpensive and suitable for curving or irregular pathways. Laying concrete is for the fit, strong and knowledgeable
WOOD & BARK		Pulverised or shredded bark has become a popular material in woodland and wild gardens. It is soft underfoot but requires topping up every few years. Sawn log rounds are sometimes set in the shredded bark
GRAVEL & PEBBLES		Gravel is by far the cheapest material. Shingle (small stones smoothed by water) and true gravel (stone chips from a quarry) are the types available. Large rounded pebbles are sometimes used for small decorative areas
PATTERN-PRINTED CONCRETE		A post-war development which is worth considering. A concrete-based mix is poured over the area and a roller is taken over the surface before it has set. The roller leaves an embossed pattern in the form of blocks, slabs or crazy paving

ADDING PLANTS

Flowers in beds and borders

Flowers in containers

Hard Landscaping Illustrated

This brick-paved front garden is both neat and practical — no lawn to mow and few plants to tend. It is, however, too severe for many people. ▷

◁ *This is the opposite approach to the garden above — here the paving slabs are swamped by a mass of annuals and it is too garish for many people.*

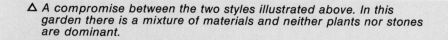

△ *A compromise between the two styles illustrated above. In this garden there is a mixture of materials and neither plants nor stones are dominant.*

GROUND COVER PLANTS

There is one fundamental difference between ground cover plants and the non-grass lawn plants such as Chamomile and Thyme described on pages 116–117. Ground cover plants will not stand up to foot traffic, and so their use is limited to those areas of ground where nobody walks. This may sound as if ground cover plants have a more restricted role to play than the non-grass lawn makers, but the opposite is true for two reasons. Some ground cover plants are very vigorous and once established will suppress virtually all weeds and need little or no attention. Next, the choice is much greater, ranging from ground hugging leafy creepers to waist-high arching conifers.

The truth is that the non-grass lawn plants provide a novel but labour-intensive and unreliable turf whereas ground cover plants provide a blanket of living colour in difficult areas and are an essential feature in countless gardens. These difficult areas are sites where grass is either hard or impossible to grow or mow. Examples are ground under leafy trees where some ground covers but not satisfactory grass can exist, and sloping banks where mowing is not possible. Most of the plants have a fairly controlled growth pattern but some are rampant invaders which can be a nuisance if the area to be covered is strictly limited. On a large bank, however, the vigorous types can be a godsend.

Labour-saving when established, perhaps, but they take both time and care at the beginning. First of all you must prepare the planting site thoroughly — all annual and perennial weeds must be killed or removed by manual or chemical means. Next, newly-planted ground cover will be surrounded by bare earth, so mulch if possible or hand pull any emerging weeds promptly for a couple of seasons. After that the plants should look after themselves apart from occasional hand weeding and any trimming which may be necessary.

In most situations the ground cover plant is the most satisfactory alternative to grass in areas where an ordinary lawn is not possible, but do not overdo it. From the design point of view it is better to have just one or perhaps a few types than a patchwork quilt of ground cover plants.

A–Z OF GROUND COVER PLANTS

NAME	PLANT TYPE	NOTES
AJUGA	Evergreen Hardy Perennial	A. reptans is a low-growing carpeting plant — blue flowers in spring. Choose one of the coloured-leaf varieties. Height 4 in. Planting distance 12 in. Propagate by division
ALCHEMILLA	Deciduous Hardy Perennial	A. mollis (Lady's Mantle) is an old favourite — attractive rounded leaves and small yellowish-green flowers in June–August. Height 9 in. Planting distance 18 in. Propagate by division
ARABIS	Evergreen Rock Garden Plant	A. caucasica (Rock Cress) forms large ground-covering mounds in sunny well-drained soil. White flowers in spring. Height 4 in. Planting distance 12 in. Propagate by cuttings or division
BALLOTA	Evergreen Hardy Perennial	B. pseudodictamnus forms stout branches with silvery-grey woolly leaves. White/purple flowers are borne in summer. Height 12 in. Planting distance 18 in. Propagate by cuttings or division
BERGENIA	Evergreen Hardy Perennial	Bergenia is slow to spread but its glossy leaves are large and it is very hardy. Pink, red, purple or white flowers appear in spring. Height 12 in. Planting distance 18 in. Propagate by division
CALLUNA	Evergreen Shrub	Scotch Heather is a satisfactory ground cover if the soil is acid and moisture-retentive. Foliage is often attractively coloured. Height 9–18 in. Planting distance 12 in. Propagate by cuttings or division
CEANOTHUS	Evergreen Shrub	You would not expect to find Ceanothus listed as ground cover, but C. thrysiflorus repens and C. Blue Mound make compàct mounds. Height 24 in. Planting distance 36 in. Propagate by cuttings
CERASTIUM	Evergreen Rock Garden Plant	A menace in the rockery but a useful rapid-spreading ground cover for a dry bank. Silvery leaves, white early summer flowers. Height 6 in. Planting distance 12 in. Propagate by cuttings, division or seed
COTONEASTER	Evergreen Shrub	Lots of showy berries and good foliage colours in autumn. Choose an evergreen variety e.g. C. Gnom or C. Skogholm. Height 4 in. Planting distance 24 in. Propagate by cuttings or division
COTULA	Evergreen Hardy Perennial	C. squalida is a low-growing carpeting plant with dense ferny foliage. Small yellow flowers appear in spring — tolerates light shade. Height 1 in. Planting distance 9 in. Propagate by division
EPIMEDIUM	Evergreen Hardy Perennial	A slow-spreading ground cover for shade — leaves turn bronze in autumn. Choose an evergreen variety such as E. perralchicum. Height 9 in. Planting distance 12 in. Propagate by division
ERICA	Evergreen Shrub	Heather is a good ground cover for free-draining sunny sites — not all need acid soil. Wide range of flowering times and colours. Height 6–18 in. Planting distance 12 in. Propagate by cuttings or division
EUONYMUS	Evergreen Shrub	The popular ones are the variegated evergreens — e.g. E. radicans Silver Queen. Woody stems bear oval leaves. Height 12 in. Planting distance 18 in. Propagate by cuttings or division
EUPHORBIA	Evergreen Hardy Perennial	Choose an evergreen species. E. robbiae will grow almost anywhere — green leathery leaves, yellow flowers in early summer. Height 12 in. Planting distance 18 in. Propagate by division or seed
GENISTA	Evergreen Shrub	Several species of this Broom can be used as ground cover — all have wiry stems and yellow flowers. G. lydia is the most popular one. Height 24 in. Planting distance 18 in. Propagate by cuttings or seed
GERANIUM	Deciduous Hardy Perennial	Some Crane's Bill varieties form clumps and can be used for ground cover — G. procumbens is a wide-spreading creeper. Height 3–24 in. Planting distance 12–18 in. Propagate by division
HALIMIOCISTUS	Evergreen Shrub	An unusual ground cover — worth considering if the site is sunny and free-draining. Spreading branches bear white flowers in summer. Height 12 in. Planting distance 18 in. Propagate by cuttings
HEBE	Evergreen Shrub	Many varieties available — dense oval leaves and bottle brush flowers in summer. Some are not fully hardy. Height 12–24 in. Planting distance 18 in. Propagate by cuttings
HEDERA	Evergreen Climber	A useful ground cover, especially in dense shade. Many leaf variegations are available in white, yellow and gold. Height 6 in. Planting distance 36 in. Propagate by cuttings or division
HEUCHERA	Evergreen Hardy Perennial	The Coral Flower has green or coloured leaves and bears tiny bell-shaped blooms (white, pink or red) on slender stems in summer. Height 24 in. Planting distance 18 in. Propagate by division
HOSTA	Deciduous Hardy Perennial	A good ground cover for partial shade — grown for its attractive foliage and spikes of white or purple flowers in summer. Height 18–24 in. Planting distance 18 in. Propagate by division

Ajuga reptans 'Variegata'

Ballota pseudodictamnus

Calluna vulgaris 'Robert Chapman'

Cotoneaster dammeri

Erica carnea 'Springwood White'

Euonymus fortunei 'Variegatus'

Euphorbia polychroma

Geranium 'Russell Pritchard'

Hosta decorata

NAME	PLANT TYPE	NOTES
HYPERICUM	Semi-evergreen Shrub	H. calycinum (St John's Wort) forms a mat of oval leaves in sun or shade. Large yellow flowers are borne in summer. Height 12 in. Planting distance 18 in. Propagate by cuttings, division or seed
IBERIS	Evergreen Rock Garden Plant	Perennial Candytuft is an attractive ground cover for a sunny well-drained site — the leaves are covered with masses of flowers in early summer. Height 9 in. Planting distance 12 in. Propagate by cuttings
JUNIPERUS	Evergreen Conifer	The prostrate and mound-forming varieties of Juniper are the most popular ground-covering conifers. Green, gold and blue available. Height 6–36 in. Planting distance 18–60 in. Propagate by cuttings
LAMIUM	Semi-evergreen Hardy Perennial	Worth considering for a shady site. The leaves have a central band of white and the white or mauve flowers appear in early summer. Height 4 in. Planting distance 12 in. Propagate by division
LAVANDULA	Evergreen Shrub	Lavender is usually thought of as a hedging plant, but some of the low-growing varieties such as L. Munstead can be used in a sunny site. Height 18 in. Planting distance 18 in. Propagate by cuttings
LIRIOPE	Evergreen Hardy Perennial	L. muscari (Lily-turf) forms clumps of grassy foliage and bears spikes of lilac flowers in late summer. Good drought resistance. Height 12 in. Planting distance 12 in. Propagate by division or seed
LONICERA	Semi-evergreen Shrub	L. pileata is a low and spreading bush with stiff branching stems. Leaves are small and glossy — fruits are purple. Tolerates shade. Height 18 in. Planting distance 18 in. Propagate by cuttings or seed
LYSIMACHIA	Deciduous Hardy Perennial	L. nummularia (Creeping Jenny) is a ground cover plant for damp soil — leaves are tiny and yellow flowers appear in summer. Height 2 in. Planting distance 12 in. Propagate by division
NEPETA	Deciduous Hardy Perennial	Catmint requires a sunny well-drained site. The grey-green leaves are aromatic and in summer there are small mauve flowers. Height 9 in. Planting distance 12 in. Propagate by cuttings or division
PACHYSANDRA	Evergreen Shrub	This prostrate plant is one of the best ground covers for growing under trees. Leaf growth is dense and white flowers appear in spring. Height 4 in. Planting distance 12 in. Propagate by cuttings or division
POLYGONUM	Evergreen Hardy Perennial	P. affine is an excellent carpeting plant which thrives in moist and shady situations. Leaves turn red in winter — flowers are pink or red. Height 6–9 in. Planting distance 9–12 in. Propagate by division
PULMONARIA	Deciduous Hardy Perennial	Lungwort is recognised by its white-spotted foliage. Flowers are blue or pink — some varieties are semi-evergreen. Height 6–12 in. Planting distance 12 in. Propagate by division
ROSA	Deciduous Shrub	A wide range of ground cover Roses are now available — there are both prostrate and bushy mound forms. Height 9–48 in. Planting distance 30–72 in. Propagate by cuttings
SAXIFRAGA	Evergreen Hardy Perennial	S. urbium (London Pride) is the one to choose — rosettes of fleshy leaves cover the ground and there are sprays of tiny pink flowers in summer. Height 3 in. Planting distance 12 in. Propagate by division
SEDUM	Evergreen Rock Garden Plant	The usual one is S. spathulifolium which has low-growing creeping stems, fleshy leaves and starry yellow flowers in summer. Height 3 in. Planting distance 9 in. Propagate by cuttings or division
SENECIO	Evergreen Shrub	Senecio 'Sunshine' is the one to choose — it is a tall ground cover with grey leaves and lots of yellow daisy-like flowers in summer. Height 36 in. Planting distance 36 in. Propagate by cuttings
STACHYS	Evergreen Hardy Perennial	S. byzantina (Lamb's Ears) has grey woolly leaves and tiny purple flowers in summer. S. Silver Carpet is a non-flowering carpeting plant. Height 4 in. Planting distance 12 in. Propagate by division
TELLIMA	Evergreen Hardy Perennial	The heart-shaped leaves are hairy and in spring the spikes of tiny bell-shaped flowers appear. Less fussy about soil and sun than Tiarella. Height 6 in. Planting distance 12 in. Propagate by division
TIARELLA	Evergreen Hardy Perennial	The Foam Flower needs damp soil in shade — the sycamore-like leaves turn reddish-bronze in winter. Spring flowers are tiny. Height 6 in. Planting distance 12 in. Propagate by division
VINCA	Evergreen Shrub	This mat-forming ground cover has creeping stems which root as they go. An excellent choice — flowers are white, blue or purple. Height 3–9 in. Planting distance 18 in. Propagate by cuttings or division
WALDSTEINIA	Evergreen Rock Garden Plant	A mat-forming plant with lobed leaves which turn golden in autumn. There are yellow flowers in spring. A grow-anywhere plant. Height 3 in. Planting distance 12 in. Propagate by division

Juniperus squamata 'Blue Star'

Lamium galeobdolon 'Variegatum'

Lavandula spica 'Hidcote'

Lysimachia nummularia 'Aurea'

Pachysandra terminalis

Polygonum affine 'Donald Lowndes'

Pulmonaria saccharata

Rosa 'Essex'

Vinca minor 'Caerulea'

CHAPTER 10

LAWN INDEX

Acknowledgements

The author wishes to acknowledge the painstaking work of Gill Jackson, Paul Norris, Linda Fensom and Angelina Gibbs. Grateful acknowledgement is also made for the help or photographs received from Joan Hessayon, Colin Bailey, Pat Brindley, Harry Smith Horticultural Photographic Collection, John Neubauer/The Garden Picture Library, La Talbooth (Dedham) and the Buckinghamshire County Museum (Aylesbury).

Artwork for this book was produced by the late John Woodbridge and Henry Barnett. Other artists who contributed were Norman Barber, John Dye, Pat Harby, Yvon Still and Brian Watson.